C.S. LEWIS

A Celebration of His Early Life

BROADMAN
& HOLMAN
PUBLISHERS

NASHVILLE, TENNESSEE

C.S. LEWIS

A Celebration of His Early Life

RUTH JAMES CORDING

[PHOTOGRAPHY AND ILLUSTRATIONS]

ROBERT CORDING

© 2000
by Ruth James Cording
Printed in the United States of America

0-8054-2200-5

Published by Broadman & Holman Publishers, Nashville, Tennessee

Dewey Decimal Classification: 823
Subject Heading: BIOGRAPHY

Library of Congress Cataloging-in-Publication Data

Cording, Ruth James, 1911-
   C. S. Lewis : a celebration of his early life / Ruth James Cording.
   p.   cm.
   Includes bibliographical references.
   ISBN 0-8054-2200-5
   1. Lewis, C. S. (Clive Staples), 1898-1963—Childhood and youth. 2. Belfast (Northern Ireland)
   —Social life and customs. 3. Authors, English—20th century—Biography. 4. Authors, Irish—
   20th century—Biography. 5. Christian biography—England. 6. Christian biography—Ireland. I. Title.

   PR6023.E926 Z64135 2000
   823'.912 — dc21
   [B]
                                                                                         99-089615

1 2 3 4 5 04 03 02 01 00

{ For Edward
(1904-1997) }

CONTENTS

"The childhood shows the man," wrote Milton in *Paradise Regained*, "as morning shows the day."[1]

C. S. Lewis acknowledged that in every biography he had read, the earlier years were by far the most interesting. In his biography *Surprised by Joy*, he felt it important to show what sort of person his childhood and adolescence had made him, so that "when the spiritual crisis arrives," the reader would understand.

When my own children were reading *The Screwtape Letters* and *Out of the Silent Planet* in school, I first became aware of the writings of C. S. Lewis. Much later, I was challenged to write about the childhood of C. S. Lewis after it was suggested that his mother could not have had much influence

in his life, though she was with him for the first ten formative years.

Having raised three children of my own, I can empathize with Flora Hamilton Lewis. This mother had nursed her baby boys and cared for them lovingly. Her letters to her husband, while on holiday, contained much about the wet weather and its effect on the children. She also had much fun and interest to share with Albert, their father, whom she affectionately addressed as "Dear Bear."

The godly heritage, from both sides of Lewis's family, was vindicated when C. S. Lewis became an outstanding advocate of faith in the Lord Jesus Christ. He said there was "a unity in his life." The childhood and the adult life were "of the same piece."[2]

While Lewis's childhood was unlike that of most of us, we catch glimpses that cause us to say in surprise, "Why, I felt like that too." He told us about his early years, and others have told us also. One relative wrote, "Jack was a remarkable boy, besides being one of the most loveable." And his beloved older brother, Warren, edited and typed the eleven-volume Lewis Papers: Memoirs of the Lewis Family, which had been assembled by their father Albert.[3] From these remarkable memoirs we find much of interest and are able to share the precious letters which their mother, Florence Hamilton Lewis, wrote while on holidays with her boys.

The outpouring of interest in the film *Shadowlands*, depicting the story of Lewis's marriage to Joy

Davidman, has precipitated new studies of this brilliant Oxford don.

More than thirty-five years ago, as archivist at Wheaton College, Wheaton, Illinois, I was handed seven letters that C. S. Lewis had written to Clyde S. Kilby, chairman of the college literature department. I was told to place these letters in the back of an archives file. Dr. Kilby began to collect more letters and several manuscripts. It was the inauguration of the work that developed into The Marion E. Wade Center of Wheaton College. We put out a few Lewis books for alumni and visitors. Researchers began to come. Owen Barfield, executor of the Lewis estate from Kent, England, visited us and agreed that "the people who are bestowing such loving care on the papers, should have them." This collection of letters now numbers more than twelve hundred, including some copies that are shared with the Bodleian Library in Oxford.

As for the books which Lewis wrote, sixty-eight are now published. He made a long and torturous journey from his childhood faith back to God and was acclaimed as one of the outstanding Christian apologists of the 20th century. A "sort of glory" has descended, and we are in debt to the man, "humble as a little child," who made righteousness readable.[4] It's appropriate to celebrate.

His books are instructive and concise, covering a wide range: scholarly, theological, science fiction, poetry, and children's literature. And

his letters are personal, joyous, compassionate, and brimming-over with
shared human feelings.

"Since my conversion it has
seemed to me that it was my partic-
ular job to teach the outside world
what all Christians believe," Lewis
wrote. He also felt that we were
meant to enjoy our Lord and, "in
Him, our friends, our food, our sleep,
our jokes and the birds' song and the
frosty sunrise," reminding us that it
was "God who made good laughter."[5]

When I transcribed one hundred
of his letters "To an American Lady,"
I truly began to appreciate this great
man. His letters to Mary Willis
Shelburne of Washington, D.C.,
brought much comfort to this elderly
poet, ill and lonely. When she asked
for his picture, he sent her one,
calling it "this undecorative object."

I saw it on the wall of her small
apartment. "His eyes follow me,"
she said.

In 1970, taking copies of
Lewis's original letters to the
department of Western Manuscripts
at the Bodleian Library in Oxford,
I was able to speak with Major
Warren Lewis. He was glad that his
brother's books were so valued in
the States. I still hear echoes of his
hearty, "Ha Ha Ha Ho Ho Ho!"
when I told him, on my way to Wales,
that the Welsh were the Irish who
could not swim. "That's a good one,"
he said, "I've never heard that before!"

Several years later my husband
Edward and I placed double-pinks
on the double grave in Headington
Quarry, Oxford, remembering with
deep gratitude both brothers —
Jack and Warren Lewis.

Having worked in the collection of Lewis letters and books since 1965. I hope to help others enjoy the vast serendipity of the anthology which he left us. Because he felt there were "no ordinary people," his extraordinary influence makes us all inspired and blessed.

November 29, 1998, was the one hundredth anniversary of C. S. Lewis's birth.

I want this book on my "coffee table" to remind me — and to share with others, through story and pictures — things about C. S. Lewis that are too good to miss, and a few reminiscences that may not be found anywhere else.

RUTH JAMES CORDING

LITTLE LEA.
CHILDHOOD HOME OF
C. S. LEWIS, BELFAST
IRELAND.

ACKNOWLEDGEMENTS

I am grateful for the friendship of Douglas Gresham and his family and have appreciated the encouragement and support of many associates over the years: Clyde and Martha Kilby, Lyle Dorsett, Peter Veltman, Paul Snezek, and Robert and Helen deVette.

My son Robert urged me to write this book and has helped immeasurably in developing the theme and in editing the work. His perseverance in creating the design, thus complementing the manuscript with his photography and illustrations has been for me a stimulating, shared experience.

Annette Victorin, writer, teacher, and fellow member of The National League of American Pen Women, Chicago Branch, wrote, after reading my brief article on the childhood of C. S. Lewis, "It should be made into a book."

My thanks go to Christopher Mitchell, director of The Marion E.

Wade Center and to Mrs. Marjorie Mead, codirector, for their generous permissions given for the use of the collection materials. Special appreciation to Leslie Stobbe for his enthusiasm and help in the development of the book.

My heart overflows with love and gratitude for Edward Cording, my husband of sixty-two years, and for his prayers. He gave many practical suggestions and the confidence to write this book. "Give it a whirl," he said. A Lewis enthusiast, he willingly listened as I read portions of the manuscript to him and seemed to delight in hearing it.

Each of my children has admired the writings of C. S. Lewis. Ed and Norma wrote and performed in a pageant of Lewis's books; Robert formed a partnership to purchase The Kilns, the Lewis home in Oxford; Margaret Cording Petty composed music for some of Lewis's epigrams. Her husband Thomas Petty, as well as the others have shown an interest in the manuscript and encouraged me to complete it. And my grandson, Evan James Cording, shares in the satisfaction that writing gives.

Most importantly, I acknowledge God's guidance and clear direction.

It has been a delight to peruse the books which C. S. Lewis read as a child; many are now in public domain or out of print. I wish to acknowledge also the following for permission to quote from their materials, published and unpublished:

The C. S. Lewis Estate Pte. Ltd. In care of Elizabeth Stevens and Curtis Brown, London, *They Stand Together*, edited by Walter Hooper © 1979, the poems "The Old Gray Mare" and "Joy."

The Marion E. Wade Center, Wheaton College, *The Lewis Papers: Memoirs of the Lewis Family, 1850-1930, Volumes II and III* and *C. S. Lewis: A Biography* by W. H. Lewis.

The Lewis Papers, Memoirs of the Lewis Family by C. S. Lewis © C. S. Lewis Pte. Ltd.

"HE IS JACKSIE"

CLIVE STAPLES LEWIS

During one of his childhood holidays when Lewis was about four years of age, he made the momentous decision to change his name. He didn't like the name "Clive," and no doubt to be called Babs and Babbins seemed beneath his dignity. He marched up to his mother one morning, put a forefinger on his chest and announced, "He is Jacksie." On the following day he still insisted on being called "Jacksie," refusing to answer to any other name. Later his name was shortened to "Jacks." Finally, he became "Jack" to his family and friends.

Much of the early childhood of C. S. Lewis was spent at Little Lea, a rambling house on the outskirts of Belfast near open, hilly farmland. Attending mainly English schools as a boy, he went on to become a scholar at University College, Oxford, and a don (or fellow) at Magdalen College.

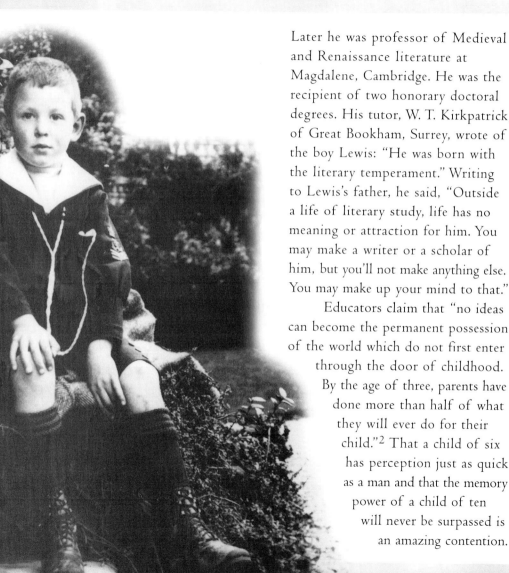

Later he was professor of Medieval and Renaissance literature at Magdalene, Cambridge. He was the recipient of two honorary doctoral degrees. His tutor, W. T. Kirkpatrick, of Great Bookham, Surrey, wrote of the boy Lewis: "He was born with the literary temperament." Writing to Lewis's father, he said, "Outside a life of literary study, life has no meaning or attraction for him. You may make a writer or a scholar of him, but you'll not make anything else. You may make up your mind to that."[1]

Educators claim that "no ideas can become the permanent possession of the world which do not first enter through the door of childhood. By the age of three, parents have done more than half of what they will ever do for their child."[2] That a child of six has perception just as quick as a man and that the memory power of a child of ten will never be surpassed is an amazing contention.

1

LITTLE LAD CHATTERING

Standing tall in his little Irish boy's suit with the large white collar, his feet planted firmly on the floor in his sturdy, one-strapped shoes, we see C. S. Lewis at five years of age. A long, braided lariat rope hangs about his neck, drapes toward his pocket, and holds a whistle at the end. Alert and interested with hair neatly combed, this little boy holds a slender rope that's tied to a white donkey with Father Christmas on its back. Later, this boy Jacksie would, as a man, dress in rumpled tweed coats with baggy gray trousers, as described by some who knew and admired him. Speaking of cast-off clothes, in a poem after the death of his beloved Charles

"The childhood shows the man as morning shows the day."[1]

— Milton

Williams, he refers to clothes as "things not needed on his journey," but thereafter on Easter Day "resume the robes he wore as a man."

What transpired since the time of the little lad chattering at his mother's knees is the remarkable story of the conversion of C. S. Lewis. It took C. S. Lewis a long time to work through the unbelief he had embraced during his young manhood. There is no doubt that the godly heritage, on both sides of the family, was vindicated as he became an outstanding advocate for faith in the Lord Jesus Christ.

"The memories of childhood have no order and no end," wrote Dylan Thomas. "The childhood shows the man," Milton writes in *Paradise Regained*, "as morning shows the day." Wordsworth wrote, "The child is father of the man," in his poem "My Heart Leaps Up."

(23)

BABY C.S. LEWIS, 1899.

LEFT: FAMILY PICTURE, ABOUT 1900. FRONT ROW: FLORA LEWIS (MOTHER); WARREN LEWIS (BROTHER); RICHARD LEWIS II (GRANDFATHER); COUSIN EILEEN; AUNT AGNES; C.S. LEWIS. BACK ROW: ALBERT JAMES LEWIS (FATHER); AND GRANDMOTHER LEWIS.

Nowhere is it more true that "the child is father of the man" than in the childhood of C. S. Lewis. Early in his life he found in himself, "A desire which no experience in this world can satisfy." This quest for joy had its roots in his childhood and continued almost to the very end of his life.

But along the way, Lewis discovered that joy was a pointer to "something other and outer"; and in finding God and the

knowledge that he was made for another world, he brought with him a host of others through his incisive, clear and Christian apologetic writings. His many books, more than fifty in all, are still popular. That this is so is a tribute to the writing skill and the faith of one of the greatest Christian minds of our time.

As a child, Lewis was made to say his prayers and attend church. His father took a natural delight in the verbal beauty of the Bible and the prayer book. But it was not until Jack went to school in Hertfordshire that for him "the doctrines of Christianity were brought to life by men who believed them." Then he began seriously to pray, to read the Bible, and to attempt to obey his conscience.

LEFT: FAMILY GROUP IN GARDEN, 1899. FROM LEFT TO RIGHT, FIRST ROW: AGNES YOUNG LEWIS (AUNT); ANNE ("ANNIE") HARLEY HAMILTON (AUNT); WARREN LEWIS, MARTHA GEE LEWIS (GRANDMOTHER); FLORA HAMILTON LEWIS (MOTHER); AND JACK LEWIS, ON MOTHER'S LAP. SECOND ROW: MARY WARREN HAMILTON (COUSIN) IN HER FATHER'S ARMS; AUGUSTUS ("GUSSIE") WARREN HAMILTON (UNCLE); LEONARD LEWIS (COUSIN); RICHARD LEWIS II (GRANDFATHER); EILEEN LEWIS (COUSIN); AND ALBERT LEWIS (FATHER).

JACKS (IN WHITE) WITH MOTHER AND COUSINS ON LAWN, NORTHERN IRELAND, CIRCA 1901.

25

"He carried a load of mischief."[1]

—Leo Baker,
Oxford friend of
C. S. Lewis

RIGHT: FAMILY GROUP, 1911.
JACK AND WARREN SIT ON EACH
SIDE OF THEIR FATHER.

THE "PROMENADE" ICE CREAM
PARLOR IN BALLYCASTLE,
IRELAND.

WE BUILT THE PROMENADE

Lewis's mother, Flora, and his father, Albert, delighted in the stories Jacksie told. In the Lewis family, a joke or a favorite story was called a "wheeze." Albert Lewis particularly enjoyed hearing and sharing his favorite wheezes, exchanging stories with the uncles. Little wonder then that he encouraged Jacksie, even before he could write, to dictate his stories to his father, usually on a Saturday evening. These stories almost all included animals as the heroes. "They got an iron pad, they built the promenade" was a sentence in one story that lingered on in the family memory for

a long time. The flyleaf inscription in his first published work in 1919, *Spirits in Bondage*, a book of poems was inscribed "To my father with the author's best love and compliments, in memory of the happy days when 'we built the Promenade' together."[2]

MRS. MOP AND THE DINNER
(April 3, 1911)

A prank that passed into family history . . . Warren and Jack were at home and having a dinner together. They were alone in the house and somehow the usual cook was not there to make the dinner. It fell to the lot of the charwoman (a word which means "the lady who obliges") to make the meal. They called her "Mrs. Mop." But the meal was a disaster — they simply could not eat it. The steak was raw, the potatoes evidently had been in warm water for only a couple of minutes. Finally the boys decided to

rebel. "Let's have a ceremonial funeral," suggested Jack. They walked in Indian file with Jack carrying the gramophone playing Chopin's Funeral March. Warnie carried the dinner and a trowel with which to bury it. They went to the flower bed outside the kitchen window. A grave was dug and the meal buried in a reverent

silence. Mrs. Mop was at the table in the kitchen. However, she was not there when the boys went later to ransack the larder. They never saw her again.[3]

— from Biography *by W. H. Lewis*

In another story the animals were defending a fortress and the leader noticed that one of his stalwarts, a duck, had fallen out. The leader reproved the duck, "Duck, this is no time for laying of eggs." Lewis's father and mother exchanged a glance before bursting into a gale of laughter. His brother Warren, who told

the story many years later, remarked that neither boy saw anything odd in the remark, and the parents refused to say what they thought was so funny.

THE CROCK OF GOLD

Jacksie was sure there was a crock of gold hidden in the middle of the drive that ran from the road to the front door.

Thick shrubbery concealed their activities from the windows on that side of the house. All afternoon they worked, Warnie doing most of the spadework. By teatime at dusk he had dug a large pit.

About an hour later the excavation was discovered by their father, coming home from business. His hat rolled one way and his bag of law papers another. Jacksie explained that they were looking for buried treasure. With a sustained torrent of harsh language, their father pointed out that they had made a dangerous booby trap for a tired man who had been struggling since morning to provide their bread and butter.

Warnie thought of telling him that they had already had their tea, "Thank you very much," but thought better of it. The boys "rode out the storm" silently but did not hear the last of it for some time.

THE TENT

Another crisis occurred when Jacksie suggested that they make a tent. They had heard that their cousin had made one with some success. With his hatchet, Warnie reduced the wash-house ladder to a number of disconnected poles. The boys planted four of them in the earth and put a dust sheet, which they had gotten from the attic, over them. Jacksie tried sitting on top which didn't work too well. Finally giving up, they put the tattered dust sheet away but forgot the uprights.

After dinner Jacksie and Warnie went for a stroll in the garden with their father. Seeing the four wooden posts, he inquired about them. They told the truth, anticipating the worst, which was not long in coming. Their father roared at them, comparing their efforts to "an abortive Punch-and-Judy Show." At his angry words they hid their faces but not to cry.

CHAPTER

MAMY IS LIKE...

orn in 1862, Florence Augusta Hamilton was a second daughter of Rev. Thomas Hamilton and Mary Warren Hamilton, daughter of Sir John Borlase Warren, a fourth baronet.[1] "Flora," as she was called, had an older sister Lilian and two brothers, Hugh and Augustus, known as "Gussie." Her father had been a Royal Navy chaplain in the Crimean War and later chaplain of Holy Trinity Church in Rome.

When Flora was twelve, her father became the rector of St. Marks Church in Dundela, Ireland. The Albert Lewis family were members of that parish and became warm friends with the younger Hamiltons. The Lewises attended the services where Flora's father

"Mamy is like most middle-aged ladys, stout, brown hair, spectaciles, kniting her shirt of industry, etc., etc."[2]

– C. S. Lewis (age 9)

With light blue eyes and fair hair, Flora, in her youth, was the very essence of an Irish colleen with "the morning freshness on her round and lovely face." From her later pictures taken with relatives, including her father-in-law, uncles, cousins, sisters-in-law, and maids, together with her husband and sons, it is easy to discern the care and attention that she gave to the establishment at Little Lea. In a family group picture we see her holding baby Clive or hovering in the background and smiling as the cousins play with her little boys. A large framed portrait of Florence Augusta Hamilton in a red velvet mat hung in the hall of The Wade Center. I was impressed to realize as I looked at the earnest, serene face that she was C. S. Lewis's mother. The high-necked ruffle set off her firm chin and intelligent eyes. The picture seemed to support the work of research and collection that was going forward in those quiet rooms, almost as if to remind us to do right by her son.

This patrician, upper-middle-class matron of Belfast stands with a group which has doubtless just returned from the services of her father's church. She is wearing a large picture hat, at least fourteen inches in diameter. She wears a surplice-like neck scarf with a pleated frill down the front that ends with points of lace. With sleeve-high long black gloves, she holds in her clasped hands a furled umbrella which speaks eloquently of the wet Irish weather.

THE RECTORY OF ST. MARKS CHURCH WHERE FLORA HAMILTON GREW UP.

36

Family group on vacation at Larne Harbour, County Antrim, Northern Ireland, 1903. From l. to r., first row: Joseph ("Joey") Lewis III (cousin); Jack Lewis, Richard Lewis II (grandfather); Leonard Lewis (cousin); and standing, Warren Lewis. Second row: Eileen Lewis (cousin); Elizabeth ("Bessie") Lewis (cousin); May Lewis (cousin); Flora Hamilton Lewis (mother); Mary Taggert Lewis (aunt); Agnes Young Lewis (aunt); Martha Lewis (cousin). Third row: Albert Lewis (father) and Joseph Lewis II (uncle).

The Welsh on the paternal side was combined with the Irish of the mother of C. S. Lewis, Florence Augusta Hamilton. Her father, the Reverend Thomas Hamilton of Belfast, had been a chaplain in the Royal Navy. He was an eloquent preacher: Her mother, Mary Warren, was aristocratic and intelligent. Through the Warrens, the ancestry went back to a Norman knight — William of Warrenne of Kipling's poem "The Land."

Lewis's great grandfather, on his mother's side, was Hugh Hamilton, a fellow of Trinity College in Dublin. He was successively dean of Armagh, bishop of Clonfert, and bishop of Ossory. An author, he published numerous books.

preached. He often wept in the pulpit during his sermon, much to the embarrassment of his daughter.

If, to some, Flora appeared cold and unemotional, she but reflected her upbringing in which her sister and brothers seemed to be more favored and noticed. Actually her family was very proud of this sensible and sunny girl, a brilliant mathematician who later took a first degree at Queen's College, Belfast, with subsequent first class honors in geometry, algebra and logic, and second class honors in mathematics.

Flora was a voracious reader, enjoying the novels of George Meredith and Leo Tolstoy, the greatest international figure of Russian literature. She began writing magazine articles and developed successful short stories.

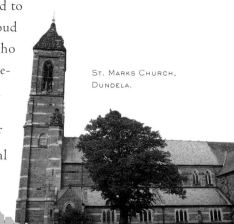

St. Marks Church, Dundela.

> *"Good parents,*
> *good food, and*
> *a garden to*
> *play in."* [4]
>
> *— C. S. Lewis*

In 1893, Flora agreed to marry Albert, but in her coolheaded and matter-of-fact way, she wrote to him, "I wonder do I love you? I know that at least I am very fond of you and that I should never think of loving anyone else. I feel it is the only real love that has ever been offered me. It will be quite a new experience for me to live with someone with whom I shall really be first. At home, I have never even been second." [3]

When Albert Lewis was courting Flora, her greatest fear seemed to be that she might not be able to return his love in kind. She wrote to him, "There is not anything about me to make me worthy of so much love as you give me. You think more of me than I deserve." Yet her warm sweet letters, after they were married, addressed to "my dear Bear," and "my dear old love," "with lots of kisses from your loving wife, Doli" disprove any such lack.

Florence Hamilton and Albert Lewis were married August 29, 1894, at St. Mark's Church, Dundela, a suburb of Belfast. The reception was at the Royal Avenue Hotel in Belfast. Albert's father, in a patriarchal prayer, asked God to bless this couple and make their children a blessing to them. Albert's wedding gift to his bride was a "Diamond Star"— jewelry worth several thousand dollars.

THE HAND HOTEL

THE RIVER WYE NEAR
TINTERN, WALES.

HONEYMOON IN WALES

For their honeymoon they took a first-class, picturesque tour of north Wales. It was Albert's wish to show the woman he loved the magnificence of the land of his fathers.

RHUDDLAN CASTLE, WALES.

A week's stay at Betws-y-coed with its Swallow and Conway Falls, deep within fairy glens, provided ideal walking country. At the mountain village of Capel Curig, they were in the shadow of mighty Snowdon, the highest mountain in all of Britain.

NORTH WALES

At Llangollen, in the beautiful River Dee Valley, they stayed at the Hand Hotel. From the village of Dolgellau, which gives fine views across the Cambrian Mountains, they could see the rugged face of Cader Idris, where later their sons, Warren and Jack, took one of their many annual walking tours.

They stopped at Bangor, the cathedral and university city of north Wales. (Years later, C.S. Lewis delivered his first lecture at Bangor University on Milton, as described in his Preface to Paradise Lost.)

BRECON BEACONS WHERE C.S. LEWIS HIKED.

CAPEL CURIG, WALES.

A ferry of the Irish Passenger Steamship Services took them back across the Irish Sea to Ireland and home.

The couple made their home in Dundela Villas (one of a pair of semidetached houses on the outskirts of Belfast, which they rented from a relative). On June 16, 1895, their first son, Warren Hamilton Lewis, was born. Three years later, on the cold, foggy afternoon of November 29, 1898, their second son, Clive Staples Lewis was born at home in Dundela Villas, Belfast, Ireland.

Flora nursed her boys in their infancy, and as they grew, she was careful of their diets, protecting them from illness and concerned for their well-being in the wet Irish weather. She not only loved them; she enjoyed them, supplying them with the drawing tools that they later used so effectively and giving them freedom to play, to choose books for themselves, and providing them with a private place of their own. She tutored them in French and Latin and they often went on long walks together. A fond mother! Could she in any way imagine what Jacksie would be when he grew up? Or the books which both he and Warren would write?

As time went on, Flora had taken on a large establishment, much more ordered and cleaner than her mother's house, with the control and scheduling of maids, cook, and gardener that were usual in an Irish household of the requirements of that day. Flora saw to it that her husband had a daily portion of the roast beef which he fancied. She was, undoubtedly, a no-nonsense woman, but compassionate withal. She believed in "all reasonable comforts" but wondered why people "worry so much about secular things."

4

I AM LIKE PAPY

*A*lbert was a favorite of Thomas and Mary Hamilton, of St. Marks Church of Ireland in Dundela, long before he began to court their daughter, Flora. He discussed politics with the rector and arranged trips for them. Although Albert told Flora of his love in 1886, she did not agree to marry him until 1893. And the wedding took place in 1894 after the year's engagement. Eight years he waited for the fair-haired Flora.

Albert James Lewis was born in Cork, Ireland, in 1862, the youngest of the six children of Richard Lewis II and Martha Gee Lewis. Richard Lewis II had emigrated to Ireland from Wales.

"I am like Papy. Bad temper, thick lips, think, and generally wearing a jersey."[1]
—C.S. Lewis

43

Albert provided a good home and good food, even the almost daily allotment of roast beef. There seemed a certain delight in luxury and in "civilization."

Lewis's father was fond of poetry and had great quickness of mind, a resonant voice, and a remarkable memory. In telling a story, he would act out all the characters in turn with appropriate gestures. He especially enjoyed Trollope's political novels.

Albert's was a legal career, and he was much sought after as a political speaker. The friends who came to his home discussed politics and money almost exclusively. The boys had to sit courteously with these visitors and listen while these subjects were put forward, although they longed to leave the room for their own projects.

Little wonder that the boy, Jacksie, and his older brother, Warren, filled their Boxen stories with stiff and arrogant political animals amid the echoes of his father's friends raving about "this rotten Liberal government." Characters such as Viscount Puddiphat, an owl; Lord John Big, a frog; and Rajah Hawki of India. Sir Charles Arabudda was a salmon who became a doctor. Years later, when referring to a doctor's appointment, C. S. Lewis mentioned that he was to see Dr. Arabudda, understood of course by his brother.

Albert Lewis found it difficult to relate to his boys, especially after their mother's death, forcing his presence upon them when they had plans of their own. "I am like Papy," wrote Jack in

WARREN, FATHER AND JACK.

45

Albert's great grandfather, Richard I, was a farmer and lived in the small town of Caergwhle, North Wales. Albert's grandfather, Joseph, was also a farmer and settled at Saltney, south of Chester, becoming a Primitive Methodist minister; later called by parishioners as "the grand old man of Methodism." His eloquent sermons displayed much fervor or "hwyl" as the Welsh call such preaching.

LEFT: MILL AT CENARTH,
TEIFI RIVER, WALES.

ALBERT LEWIS.

47

BELMONT AVENUE NEAR
DUNDELA FLATS.

the briefly kept diary in 1907. "Bad temper, thick lips, thin, and generally wearing a jersey."

At first his sons feared him because he would turn a disciplinary word into an occasion for the most exaggerated lecturing. But, in the end, his forgiveness was thorough-going.

As the boys grew older, they came to realize the humor of his rhetoric during what should have been a simple scolding. Still later they came to realize what an excellent raconteur their father was, for no one could tell a story better.

The unsettling sadness that came into the lives of Jack and Warnie Lewis with the death of their mother was increased by the overwhelming grief of their father, Albert, at the loss of his wife. Unable to understand his often-uncontrolled emotions and temper, the boys pulled away from him, drawing closer to each other.

In Albert's attempts to take their mother's place, it seems he often blundered. He sent Jack away to a boarding school in England, which brought much unhappiness to the young boy. Later, however, he entrusted his son to the tutelage of his friend William T. Kirkpatrick. Here Jack blossomed, somewhat fulfilling the dream his father had for his future.

In later years Jack expressed much appreciation to his father for his support during his early schooling. But often the communication between them failed.

Reconciliation did come at last, and Jack felt he understood his father. When Albert was ill, Jack went to him and cared for him during his last illness. His father died in September 1929. His death reinforced Jack's belief in immortality and the fact that often "a great good" comes to the grieving ones after the death of a beloved member of the family.

BELFAST SKYLINE.

FLORA'S LETTERS

50

o one can doubt the influence which C. S. Lewis's mother had on him, though she died when he was ten. Her love and caring are shown in her priceless letters.

Here are excerpts from some of the delightful letters Flora wrote to her husband, Albert, whom she affectionately called "Dear Bear," while she and the children were on several annual holidays to the seaside.

With these letters in juxtaposition are placed portions from Lewis's later writings that present surprising parallels. This is borne out in Lewis's statement that his childhood was "in unity with the rest of his life."[2]

On holidays, Flora Lewis took her children and a maid to seaside resorts in County Antrim and County Down with

RAIL TRACKS AT CASTLEROCK.

FARMHOUSE ON THE COAST.

51

the picturesque names of "Ballycastle" and "Castlerock."
That this mother loved, cared for, and encouraged her two
little boys is delightfully revealed in the letters compiled by
Major Warren Lewis, the older brother of C. S. Lewis, in
his unpublished *Memoirs of the Lewis Family*.

The annual seaside holiday with their mother was

BALLYCASTLE

19th June 1900

Dear Bear,

I know I should have written a line yesterday, but I really could not fit it in; in the morning Baby had a sort of cold, and it was damp and we could not go out, so he was cross and I just had to amuse him all the time. . . . I am writing this after dinner with Babs muddling about, and he knocks up against me now and then, so you must not mind the writing being bad. . . . He was hoarse yesterday and today his mouth is watering all the time and he is ever so cross, so I suppose it is his teeth.

Flora

POST OFFICE AT BALLYCASTLE.
RIGHT: SHORELINE EAST OF BALLYCASTLE.

"Babsie is talking like anything."

BALLYCASTLE

6th August 1900

I ought to have written to you yesterday, but . . . it poured all day, and you know what that means, the children all over you all the time. . . . Babsie is talking like anything. He astonished me this morning; Warren sniffled and he turned round and said, "Warnie wipe nose." . . . He asks for you often, and thinks that men he sees passing in grey coats are Pappy. . . . He is quite reconciled to the piano.

the real highlight of their childhood years. After selecting their toys and the packing was done, they rode behind a horse in a cab to the station. This was all very exciting, but the train ride from Belfast and up the coast road was best of all. Their first view of the sea was exhilarating.

Their father, Albert, remained at home, however, continuing his business duties. He would visit them only occasionally on weekends. Thus we have the wonderful holiday letters that Flora wrote to her husband.

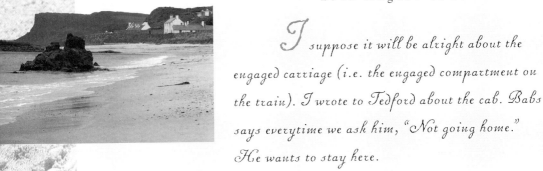

BALLYCASTLE
27th August 1900

I suppose it will be alright about the engaged carriage (i.e. the engaged compartment on the train). I wrote to Tedford about the cab. Babs says everytime we ask him, "Not going home." He wants to stay here.

". . . baby much concerned because he cannot find a crab."

CASTLEROCK
June 1901

We got down very comfortably last night. Babbins was delighted with the train . . . they were both down on the sand all the morning, baby much concerned because he cannot find a crab; also very anxious to go into the water, but I can't let him go until his cough is a bit better.

54

> "... he is much concerned because the
> postman does not bring him a letter."

CASTLEROCK
10th June 1901

On Sunday, it rained heavily, and today is very showery.
Still, we get out between while and keep either near the station or the
house so as not to get caught. . . . The children have a salt warm bath
every night. I give a little girl a penny to bring up a bucket of salt
water. . . . Look in the bathroom or my room if you can see a small
cardboard box with the precious "Miss Noah" in it, also the paint
brush, we meant most particularly to bring them . . . and of course
when it was wet yesterday they were the only things Baby wanted.
Address them to him, as he is much concerned
because the postman does
not bring him a letter.

LEFT: LOOKING EAST FROM BALLYCASTLE.
SALMON COTTAGE — KENBANE.

*"Baby doesn't see any string
on the engines...."*

CASTLEROCK
17th June 1901

When you come down bring a warm coat, as it is really cold, and I will let you bring my tweed coat also. . . . Here is a little story of Babbins to amuse the old people.[3] I took him into a shop to buy a penny engine and the woman asked him if she should tie a string to it for him. Baby just looked at her with great contempt and said, "Baby doesn't see any string on the engines that Baby sees in the station." You never saw a woman so taken aback. He is just infatuated with the trains; no matter where he is, if he sees a "siglan" down he has to be taken back to the station. . . . He had a bad night with his teeth last night.

"I was, I believe an intolerable chatterbox, (I talked to) parents; Grandfather Lewis, prematurely old and deaf, the maids, and a somewhat bibulous old gardener."[4]

Who could have predicted that his talks on BBC many years later would be heard by more than six hundred thousand people — talks which later were published in his book *Mere Christianity*.

"Baby spent most of the day making his man catch fish by the primitive method."

CASTLEROCK

Friday morning. (undated)

Yesterday was a dreadful day, poured and blew all day, such wind I never heard in my life before. . . . As I had to go out I bought the children two little boats with men in them; we made paper fishes, and Baby spent most of the day making his man catch fish by the primitive method of jumping over the side and bringing the fish back with him. . . . The place suits Babs well. . . . I am ashamed to confess, after giving you so much trouble, that Miss Noah has turned up. She was in a carriage of one of the trains. I am glad we found her, as Baby does not seem to enjoy his games without her. . . . He has made great friends with the Station Master; he went up with me today to get the papers, and as soon as he saw him in the distance he called out "Hullo Station Master." The station is being painted now, so you will understand how attractive it is to the children.

CASTLEROCK
6th July 1901

*W*e had Babbins in wading the other day and he was simply delighted with it; only he was quite too adventuresome and would walk in as far as we let him, without a hand. . . . I would like to take him for a dip, but no doubt it would not be wise while he is still coughing. He howled when we put his boots on again.

CASTLEROCK
10th July 1901

*W*e had some three or four claps of thunder after dinner. Poor Babbins, whose first experience it was, was very much frightened, he sat on Lizzie's knees with his face hidden till long after it was all over, and had to be taken down to the kitchen for a cup of tea before he could get over it. Then he told us that he thought it was his nursery falling down. Poor Warren, who had never said a word, told me today that he had been frightened too, but when he saw how Babs was, did not like to say anything for fear of making him worse, which was really very nice of him.

CASTLEROCK
24th July 1901

I think we shall have to decide to come by the train, leaving here at 3:30; it is rather slow and the one at 11:30 is quicker, but that would mean the children getting no regular dinner and Babs, I'm afraid, would be very cross without it; he takes a fine dinner now, vegetables, soup, and everything, and he comes up from it with a satisfied air of repletion which is very funny. . . . He insists on saying, "Good morning Robert" to the Station Master every morning, and gets a smile in return.

Being concerned that the postman hadn't brought him a letter! How significant that this master-correspondent was later to receive hundreds of letters and always felt that it was his Christian duty to answer them, which he usually did in longhand.

"Christmas mails have 'got me down.' This season is to me mainly hard gruelling work . . . write, write, write, till I wickedly say that if there were less good will (going through the post) there would be more peace on earth."[5]

"To be called Babs and Babbins seemed beneath his dignity. He marched up to his mother one morning, put a forefinger on his chest and announced, 'He is Jacksie.'"

SPAR HOTEL, BALLYAHINCH, CO. DOWN
11th May 1903

We had a very poor time of it on Saturday and Sunday, rain and Northeast winds all day. . . . Jacksie asks everyday if I think you will remember to buy him a set of chessmen; he is particularly anxious that they should have "whirly whirly bodies. . . ." Warren drew and then cut out a whole set of men, and we made a board out of one of the drawing blocks on which I showed them the moves; they picked it up really wonderfully and took a great interest in it.

ABOVE BALLINTOY HARBOUR.

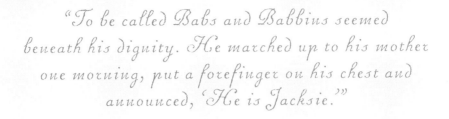

> *"Jacksie and Warren are in one room . . . and their window looks out on the railway. . . ."*

CLIFTON TERRACE, CASTLEROCK
Saturday 1904

We had a comfortable journey yesterday, and the boys were very good. . . . It has been very wet this morning, but it is clearing up now. Of course this has been a bothersome morning with the children, who nag on about wading, etc., which cannot be done in the rain. Jacksie and Warren are in one room . . . and their window looks out on the railway . . . and I had to get up at four this morning. They pulled up the blind and were settling themselves to a morning's fun, but I got them to go to sleep again. . . . They are anxious about the rabbit, and send their love. . . .

I had to get up to Jacksie 3 or 4 times. I think he did not like the dark. Jacksie's bed is the best and he said he was quite comfortable.

He had a bilious turn.

I gave him some syrup of figs — set him alright again.

The boys have set their heart on walking to Downhill this afternoon. I am writing this on my knee as the dinner is on one end of the table and the children are playing on the other end. J. would be alright if he were let alone. Warren teases Jacksie.

> *"I shall be very, very glad to be back with my dear Bear in our own home next week."*

CLIFTON TERRACE, CASTLEROCK
26th August 1904

My dear old love,

I am anxious to get up to see the house, I expect to see a great difference. Poor Jacks has never been up since there was anything to see. [This refers to "the new house," Little Lea, which was being built and to which they moved in the spring of 1905.] Jacks is concerned that his father is not getting a holiday for his birthday.

Warren is wild about fishing. He only got three the size of sardines in a landing net. He tried with a hook and a crab or something ran away with the hook.

I am not exactly tired of Castlerock, but I am lonely and shall be very, very glad to be back with my dear BEAR in our own home next week. Martha will have a fire in the nursery and blankets and sheets well-aired.

*With lots of Kisses
From your loving wife, Doli.*

DUNES AND OCEANFRONT RESORTS AT CASTLEROCK.

CASTLEROCK
Wednesday

The boys are very well, and do enjoy themselves here. . . . They bathed together and had the greatest fun; Jacks was delighted with it, and looks so funny skipping round in his bathing drawers. . . . Now that I have a nightlight they never wake at night. . . . I let them stay up until 8:30 and they go to sleep in about five minutes. They don't wake up until the first train in the morning, about 6:30, which has them out of bed like a shot.

CLIFTON TERRACE, CASTLEROCK
22nd August, 1904

Jacksie's foot looks to me to be more swelled than it was, but he does not complain about it hurting him and of course, he runs about the whole time, which can't be good for it. We are thinking of going to Derry to see walls and old cannons.

"London is a lovely place."

PENSION PETIT-VALLON, BERNEVAL, PRES DIEPPE

20th August, 1907

Jacks is delighted with Trafalgar Square, and the green squares all about, he says London is a lovely place. . . . We took a bus up to the Zoo, they were both delighted with the animals, and we actually saw some mice which were almost the same as common ones. I think Jacks was as pleased with them as with anything we saw. . . . I need not tell you that we were all pretty tired and feel quite sore. . . .

ON THE COAST ROAD —
LARNE HARBOUR.

When in 1922 Lewis was coming back to faith in God, he wrote of that time: "So the Great Angler played his fish and I never dreamed that the hook was in my tongue."[6]

DOWNTOWN BALLYCASTLE.

In his autobiography, *Surprised by Joy*, Lewis entitled one chapter "Check" and another "Checkmate" and likened his conversion to a chess game in which he indicates the various moves, concluding with the fourth move when his pieces "all over the board were in the most disadvantageous positions. Soon I could no longer cherish even the illusion that the initiative lay with me. My Adversary [the Lord] began to make His final moves."[7]

Years later after reading these letters, which his brother had collected, Jack Lewis commented on the fact that, as children in 1904, they couldn't go out in the rains. A child thirty years later would have been dressed in oilskins and gum boots and so'westers and could play happily on the sands in wet weather. For that only, he envied the modern child.

In May 1907, Jacks wrote to his brother at school that his mother had decided they would spend their next holiday in France. First they went to London, where Jacks was fascinated by the Tower of London.

The boys enjoyed Berneval but as the residents of the Pension were all English, they got little French. On the return to Belfast while Jacks was having lunch at Mountbracken, his cousin Quartus asked if he learned any of the language. "Yes," he replied, "*C'est defendu* means 'it is forbidden.'"

IT WAS THE FIRST BEAUTY

*A*n absence of beauty seemed to be a characteristic of Lewis's childhood. There were no attractive pictures on the walls of Little Lea. One precious "joy" however, came to him suddenly without warning when he was standing beside a currant bush on a summer day. There came to memory that earlier morning at their old home at Dundela Villas when his brother had brought in his toy garden. It was like a miniature forest, placed in the lid of a biscuit tin, covered with moss and garnished with twigs and flowers. "It was," he said, "the first beauty I ever knew," and it gave him not only a sense of nature — cool, dewy, fresh, and exuberant, but also a sense of "the great bliss of Eden." It came as "an idea of eternity," for as early as the age of six, Jacksie had felt a longing for he knew

RIGHT: LITTLE LEA, BOYHOOD
HOME OF C.S. LEWIS. BELFAST,
IRELAND.

not what. "In a sense," he wrote later, "everything else that had ever happened to me was insignificant by comparison." Throughout his life, Lewis experienced this longing and the joy that fulfilled it, which could be equated with "mystical experiences of the presence of God."[2]

The brothers had a day room in the attic of Little Lea "less like a large house than a city," instead of day-nursery and bedroom combined. Also a "little end room" which gave him "glorious privacy." Lewis was later to write "I am a product of long corridors, empty sunlit rooms, upstairs indoor silences, attics explored in solitude, distant noises of gurgling cisterns and pipes, and the noise of wind under the tiles. Also of endless books."[3]

His father bought all the books he read and never got rid of any of them. There were books in the study, books in the drawing room, books in the cloakroom, books two deep in the great bookcase on the landing, books in the bedrooms, books piled high in the attic, books readable and unreadable, books suitable for a child and books most emphatically not. "Nothing was forbidden me. In the seemingly endless rainy afternoon I took volume after volume from the shelves," said C. S. Lewis.

"In a sense, everything else that had ever happened to me was insignificant by comparison."[1]
— C. S. Lewis

67

MY BROTHER'S GIFTS

"My brother's gifts began to develop in those early days."[1]

— *Warren Lewis*

*T*he physical defect which drove Lewis to write, even as a child, was his thumb! Inherited from his father, his thumb had only one joint, being unable to bend the upper joint (that furthest away from the nail). It made him unable to make things with his hands and led to frustrating tears in his efforts with the scissors in trying to build a cardboard house or ship or engine. But with a pencil or pen, inkpot, brush and paintbox, he could deal with it, and he found that writing and illustrating a story was even more satisfying.[2] In one of the attics of Little Lea, he made his "study" and there, to his great delight, worked on the stories of Animal-Land, using every

STAIRCASE TO
THE 3RD FLOOR
AT LITTLE LEA.

69

color in his paintbox. They drew dressed animals and knights in armor and finally a map related to his brother's "India" characters in that world, prosaic and proper, were all very different from the Narnia chronicles, which Lewis would write later

There in a corner of the attic, Jacksie had a stack of pictures, his drawings, and stories which he considered his treasure.

Cupboard-like doors opened into huge dark wasted spaces under the roof. In October 1905, when Warren was at school in England, he wrote asking, "How is the secret dark hole upstairs getting on? Have you been in it lately?" And to his father Warren wrote, "How is Binks? When I come, I hope to have a nice story of his."

Many of the drawings and much of the creativeness of the Boxen stories, that imaginary country which was to be their joy for years to come, came because Jacksie and Warren were kept indoors on the many long wet days in Ireland. They amused themselves with the chalks and paint brushes which their parents generously supplied.

Because of the very real threat of tuberculosis, they were forbidden to leave the house or play in the garden on wet days. To be caught out in a shower without an overcoat was a minor disaster that required a change of clothes as soon as they were back in the house. With good reason, parents were nervous and protected the children from the dampness and exposure, since the disease in that day caused many deaths.[3]

The invention of nicknames was a source of much fun and originality to the Lewis brothers. In the northern Irish accent, potatoes were called "pudaitas." Their father slipped into the vernacular once and ever after his sons secretly called him "Pudaita" or "Pudaitabird" and used the initial "P" in their letters to each other to refer to him. It was not so much disrespect as a secret code they had between them for their father.

"Pigiebothams" were idlers who approved of their idleness. The word came from their nurse, Lizzie Endicott, threatening to "smack their pigiebottams," if they didn't behave. The "Arch Pigiebothams" (APB) was Warren; Jacks was the small "Pigiebothams" (SPB).

The genius of "naming" showed up in the titles and characters of Lewis's books.

The reflections of Jacksie's older brother, Warren, in both his autobiography and the *Memoir of the Lewis Family*, give quite a complete picture of the way it was. As a participant and as a loving and observant witness, Warren, in his writings, adds appreciably to our knowledge. He wrote, "My brother's gifts began to develop in those early days and it may not be fanciful to see, in that childhood staring out to unattainable hills, some first beginnings of a vision and viewpoint that ran through the work of his maturity.[4] It seems to me a sufficiently creditable production for a boy of eight to include 'The Old Gray Mare' poem in the *Memoir*":[5]

THE OLD GRAY MARE

Round about the lady's bower,
Round about the miller's tower,
Neath the shield
     and
O'er the field
Goes the old gray mare.

Rushing in some dreadful fray,
She's a living shield I say,
Rushing o'er the bloody field
She will face the foeman's shield.

Dash against some warhorse strange
Midst a battle's bloody throng.
Though her rider dight in steels
The heavy thing she never feels

When the bloody battle's over
Then is victory the rover.
For her feet there is the fen,
For her company the wren.
Far are known Knighthood,
But still more noble is the brood
Of the old gray mare.

Round about the miller's tower,
Round about the lady's bower,
Neath the shield
     and
O'er the field
Goes the old gray mare.

GROWING UP

DOWNTOWN BELFAST.

 As a child Lewis thought that all the mountains in the view from their home looked like mountains in a fairy story. He passionately loved those hills of County Down all his life. The Castlereagh Hills, or "Green Hills" as they were called, were "unattainable" to him as a child so often shut in because of the wet weather. However, they could see the summer sunsets behind the blue ridges and the rooks flying home.

From their front door they could see the harbor of Belfast Lough and the long line of the Antrim shore, hearing the whistles and bells of the harbor boats. On one side of Little Lea was the beginning of real country — the open hilly farmland of the Holywood Hills. On the other side they were only a short twenty-minute walk to the tram stop.

RIGHT: JACK, WARREN, ALBERT AND A NEIGHBOR.

BELFAST HARBOR FROM THE DIRECTION OF LITTLE LEA.

re than anything I'm grateful that on I'm descended from Welsh farmer."[1]

— C. S. Lewis

, Peter, white mouse named Tommy. Maude, the housemaid, and Martha, the cook, were also friends of Jacksie.

Other glimpses of Lewis's childhood come to us from the account he wrote, "My life during the Exmas holydays of 1907." He tells of their postman, Gordon, "a very nice and sensible man who sets me essays to write." He speaks of his governess, Miss Harper, who is "fairly nice for a governess." (As an adult Lewis was to praise Presbyterian Annie Harper for keeping him from snobbery.) Nurse Lizzie Endicott ("nothing but kindness, gaiety and good sense") told him stories of leprechauns with pots of gold.

Less than a mile from Little Lea stood Mountbracken, where Flora's cousins lived. Sir William Quartus Ewart and Lady Mary Ewart, his mother's dearest friend, were gracious and deeply religious people. They made Jack and Warren feel at home, almost as much as in their own house, except that a certain standard of manners had to be kept up. It was here among these loving relatives that Lewis credits his learning courtesy and self-assurance. The three daughters, Hope, Kels and Gundreda were all "grown-up," older than the boys, but nevertheless took a real interest in them. They would take Warren and Jacksie out in a donkey trap for rides, pulled by a rather obstinate donkey by the name of Grisella.[2] Glenmacken, as the house was known, was a friendly haven to which the boys would ride on their bicycles.

All Hallows Eve (Halloween) at Little Lea was celebrated with festivity and fun. They got their grandfather down from his rooms to watch, and he even tried to bite into the apple which they had hung. Inside an apple dumpling was a button, a ring and a three-penny bit. Martha, the cook, got the button, Jacks got the ring and the threepence all in one bite. Maude, the housemaid, got nothing.

In some ways the celebration was like the Fourth of July in America. There were fireworks, rockets, catterine wheels, and sparklers which, when lit, were twirled and made stars.

In December, Uncle Gussie's whole family was invited for Christmas turkey and plum pudding at Little Lea. He was Flora's brother. Augustus Hamilton and his Canadian wife, Annie, were favorites in the Lewis household. Their daughter Ruth, a cousin only two years younger than Jack, remembers sitting in the wardrobe with Jack telling stories. She thought her Aunt Flora a very clever woman and remembered the nice dinners. She liked Uncle Allie too, who told them of Chesterton's "Father Brown" stories. The boys played the gramophone for their entertainment, as they sat by the coal fire, replenished by a housemaid.

Ruth commented that she never saw "such devotion between brothers — a wonderful thing." After their mother died, Aunt Annie, Ruth's mother, helped with Warnie and Jack's clothes and tried to take their mother's place.

Richard II, Jack's grandfather, emigrated to Ireland from Wales in the 1850s. He was a master boilermaker and manager in a shipbuilding firm. His father, Joseph, was a farmer and later became a Methodist minister, settling at Saltney, south of Chester. Lewis's great, great grandfather was Richard I, born in Caergwrle (pronounced Caregooley) and buried in North Wales.

As an adult Lewis was to write:

I'm more Welsh than anything and for more

than anything in my ancestry, I'm grateful that on my

father's side I'm descended from a practical Welsh

farmer. To that link with the soil I owe whatever

measure of physical energy and stability I have, without

it I would have turned into a hopeless neurotic.

There was a very marked and unique bond between Grandfather Lewis and nine-year-old Jacksie. Having broken up his old home "Sandycroft" in 1903, the old man, Albert's father, divided his time among his sons. He lived at Little Lea in 1907 and was given the bed-sitting room which later became "the little end room" for Warnie and Jack. Relatives and friends noted how very good Flora was to her father-in-law, who had become somewhat senile. "He does not know what he is doing half of the time,"

Flora confided to her husband. But they gave Richard Lewis, still strong-willed and independent, the security of their home and loving care and affection.

The grandfather had, in turn, been a boilermaker at Cork; a yard manager in Dublin and a partner in a ship-building firm at Belfast. He was deaf, slow-moving, and concerned for his health. It was to be the last year of his life, but it was considerably brightened by the lively boy, his grandson Jack. The grandfather's stories intrigued the young Lewis, especially the tale of his "running away to sea." His father was a Primitive Methodist minister in North Wales at Mould, five miles northeast of Caergwrle. The Richard Lewis who began the line was a farmer in Caergwrle, the great, great grandfather of C. S. Lewis.

The old man and the little boy became fast friends. Grandfather Lewis had a very high opinion of the literary abilities which he saw in the child and hoped Jacksie would one day write up the stories told of his life.

Many of the essays Richard Lewis had written were of a theological nature in which he endeavored to help the fellows in the Trade Union. One of these, "Our Father at the Helm of the Universe," was placed in the workmen's reading room of the steamship company, an action his stalwart, evangelical father would doubtless have approved.

When Jacksie was describing the battles in his own Boxen stories, Grandfather Lewis remonstrated, "But our God is a God of peace." Warren was away at Wynard School in England, so Jacksie spent many hours with his grandfather. Some of the stories were forgotten, but the dramatic tale of "running away to sea," though it may have been a very brief experience, really impressed him.

Jack Lewis was to remember his grandfather reading good books, decapitating dandelions with his cane when out for a walk, and standing at a window, looking out and singing in a high and tremulous voice the psalms and hymns he had learned as a boy.[3]

"Moments where you were too happy to speak,

where the gods and heroes rioted through your head,

where satyrs danced and maenads roared on the mountains. . . .

Where heroines were all about you,

till sometimes you felt that it might

break you with mere richness." [4]

BOOKS THAT PLEASED

Many of the books and stories that pleased C. S. Lewis as a child pleased him as an adult also. He liked the bodies of books; the setup of the page and the sounds as the leaves were turned. He liked the feel of the paper, even the smell of it!

E. Nesbit's books gave him the concept of antiquity and the mystery of enchanted castles and lands.[2] In *Beatrix Potter's* books he found beauty. *Squirrel Nutkin*, however, troubled him with the season of autumn, that showed the decline of the year. He could trace big things in his thinking that went back to very small sources.

"GULLIVER'S TRAVELS"—
ADAPTED FROM AN ILLUSTRATION
BY C. MORTEN.

The *Blue Flower* by Henry Van Dyke revealed "the imaginative wonder of boyhood days." *Gulliver's Travels* by Jonathan Swift was one of his favorites.

The old *Punch* magazines showed him pictures by the illustrator Tenniel of "dressed animals," such as the Russian Bear, British Lion, and Egyptian Crocodile. The first book of Milton's *Paradise Lost* he read before he was ten years old. Years later he wrote a preface to *Paradise Lost*, an excellent introduction to Milton's poems.

Influenced by the Arthurian stories, he was disappointed at never having had a suit of armor. ("I am carpentring at a sword," he wrote to his brother.) *Sir Nigel*, by Conan Doyle and Mark Twain's *A Connecticut Yankee in King Arthur's Court* made the knights, who battled evil, very real to him.

There is no doubt that the books which children read often have a profound influence on their thinking, even in later years. And in the case of C. S. Lewis, who had such an amazing literary sense and retention of ideas and images, one can trace the results of the strong impressions of his youth. He is quick to tell us in his autobiography *Surprised by Joy* of "being uplifted into huge regions of Northern sky" and desiring the joy which his reading of Longfellow's "Saga of King Olaf" elicited.

Twilight of the Gods, with Arthur Rackham's illustrations, gave him that "wonderful reawakening" that comes after childhood is complete.

Sigurd the Volsung, *Siegfried* and *The Heroes of Asgard*, together with Matthew Arnold's *Balder Dead* brought powerful images to his reading.

THE BLUE FLOWER
by HENRY VAN DYKE

THIS BOOK REVEALED FOR LEWIS
"THE IMAGINATIVE WONDER" OF BOYHOOD DAYS.

The parents were abed and sleeping. The clock on the wall ticked loudly and lazily as if it had time to spare. Outside the rattling windows there was a restless, whispering wind. The room grew light, and dark, and wondrous lights again, as the moon played hide-and-seek through the clouds. The boy, wide awake and quiet in his bed, was thinking of the Stranger and his stories.

"It was not what he told me about the treasures," he said to himself, "that was not the thing which filled me with so strange a longing. I am not greedy for riches. But the blue flower is what I long for. I can think of nothing else. Never have I felt so before. It seems as if I had been dreaming until now — or as if I had just slept over into a new world."[3]

Lewis writes of "acres of blue flowers" after Aslan comes back to life from "the stone table" in *The Lion, the Witch and the Wardrobe*.

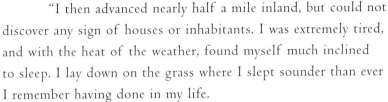

GULLIVER'S TRAVELS
by JONATHAN SWIFT
A GREAT FAVORITE OF C. S. LEWIS

"GULLIVER'S TRAVELS"—
ADAPTED FROM AN ILLUSTRATION
BY C. MORTEN.

"I then advanced nearly half a mile inland, but could not discover any sign of houses or inhabitants. I was extremely tired, and with the heat of the weather, found myself much inclined to sleep. I lay down on the grass where I slept sounder than ever I remember having done in my life.

"When I awoke, it was just daylight. I attempted to rise, but was not able to stir — for I found my arms and legs were strongly fastened on each side to the ground, and my hair, which was long and thick, tied down in the same manner. I heard confused voices about me, but I could see nothing except the sky."

Shipwrecked near the kingdom of Lilliput, Lemuel Gulliver awakened to find himself surrounded by hundreds of tiny people, none more than six inches tall. The Lilliputians take the "man-mountain" prisoner, and Gulliver learns to live in their miniature world, where he can eat three loaves of bread in a mouthful and children can play hide-and-seek in his hair!

Eventually Gulliver escapes from Lilliput and returns home. But soon he longs for further adventure and so sets sail once again. On this journey, Gulliver finds himself in Brobdingnag — a country of giants, where this time he is a pocket-sized oddity, small enough to use a handkerchief as a blanket.

"To hear some critics, one would suppose that a man had to lose his nursery appreciation of Gulliver before he acquired his mature appreciation of it. It is not so. If it were, the whole concept of maturity, of ripening, would be out of place."[4]

A CONNECTICUT YANKEE IN KING ARTHUR'S COURT
by MARK TWAIN

THE BOOK THAT MADE THE KNIGHTS REAL TO C. S. LEWIS

"CONNECTICUT YANKEE"— ADAPTED FROM AN ILLUSTRATION BY HENRY PITZ.

Hank Morgan, cracked on the head by a crowbar in nineteenth-century Connecticut, wakes to find himself in King Arthur's England. The tough-minded Yankee, an embodiment of scientific enlightenment, faces a world whose idyllic surface only masks the dark forces of fear, injustice, and ignorance. This is the springboard which launches one of literature's most extraordinary excursions into fantasy. With the agility of Mark Twain's unique virtuosity, this acrobatic *tour de force* moves from broad comedy to biting social satire and from the pure joy of wild high-jinks to deeply probing insights into human nature with its capacity for progress matched only by his capacity for destruction.

"It was during a misunderstanding conducted with crowbars with a fellow we used to call Hercules. He laid me out with a crusher alongside the head that made everything crack, and seemed to spring every joint in my skull and make it overlap its neighbor. Then the world went out in darkness, and I didn't feel anything more, and didn't know anything at all — at least for a while.

When I came to again, I was sitting under an oak tree, on the grass, with a whole beautiful and broad country landscape all to myself — nearly. Not entirely; for there was a fellow on a horse, looking down at me — a fellow fresh out of a picture book. He was in an old-time iron armor from head to heel, with a helmet on his head in the shape of a nail keg with slits in it; and he had a shield and a sword, and a prodigious spear; and his horse had armor on, too, and a steel horn projecting from his forehead, and gorgeous red and green silk trappings that hung down all around him like a bed quilt, nearly to the ground."

THE SAGA OF KING OLAF
by HENRY WADSWORTH LONGFELLOW

The Challenge of Thor

I am the God Thor,
I am the War God,
I am the Thunderer!

Here in my Northland,
My fastness and fortress,
Reign I forever!

Force rules the world still,
Has ruled it, shall rule it;
Meekness is weakness,
Strength is triumphant,
Over the whole earth
Still is it Thor's-Day!

Thou art a God too,
O Galilean!
And thus single-handed
Unto the combat,
Gauntlet or Gospel,
Here I defy thee!

Raud the Strong

"All the old gods are dead,
All the wild warlocks fled;
But the White Christ lives and reigns,
And throughout my wide domains
His Gospel shall be spread!"
On the Evangelists
Thus swore King Olaf.
But still in dreams of the night

Beheld he the crimson light,
And heard the voice that defied
Him who was crucified,
And challenged him to the fight.
To Sigurd the Bishop
King Olaf confessed it.

And Sigurd the Bishop said,
"The old gods are not dead,
For the great Thor still reigns,
And among the Jarls and Thanes
The old witchcraft still is spread."
Thus to King Olaf
Said Sigurd the Bishop.

"'T'is the warlock! It is the demon
Raud!" cried Sigurd to the seamen;
"But the Lord is not affrighted
By the witchcraft of his foes."

To the ship's bow he ascended,
By his choristers attended,
Round him were the tapers lighted,
And the sacred incense rose.

On the bow stood Bishop Sigurd,
In his robes, as one transfigured,
And the Crucifix he planted

High amid the rain and mist.

Then with holy water sprinkled
All the ship; the mass-bells tinkled;
Loud the monks around him chanted,
Loud he read the Evangelist.

As into the Fiord they darted.
On each side the water parted;
Down a path like silver milten
Steadily rowed King Olaf's ships.

In the Norse stories of *Balder and the Twilight of the Gods*, there are deep parallels between myth and reality. Balder was considered the white God, the beautiful, the just and benignant. The early Christian missionaries found him to resemble Christ in their lore — the sun god who had eclipsed the evil Loki, the fire god. The sun god was pure and radiant, full of innocence and light. His death was almost prophetic because of the resemblance to the true Christ who did die.

Lewis found the unrhymed translation of Tegner's Drapa and read:

I heard a voice that cried,
"Balder the beautiful
Is dead, is dead!"
And through the misty air

Passed like the mournful cry
Of sunward sailing cranes.

The story of Balder, in which evil seeks to triumph over the good, impressed Lewis. The folk tales of "the dying god," already familiar to him, became the touchstone for his belief. When faced with the real story of "the dying God," the sacrificial death of Christ on the cross, he finally was led to accept the Lord Jesus Christ in all sincerity. In *The Lion, the Witch and the Wardrobe*, he shows Aslan, the Lion, as the Christ-figure — bound, slain and risen again, using the children's fairy story as the channel for the real story. He believed that coming to the story in that way, without a set frame of mind, was very effective, thus putting forth "The True Myth" in all its magnificence and power.

Lewis said that "long since the gods of Asgard," God had taught him how a thing can be revered not for what it could do for him, but for what it is in itself. "God is to be obeyed," he wrote, "because of what He is Himself. The answer is 'I Am.'"[5]

With the death of Balder came the twilight of the gods. Ages passed, and Balder never returned. Then time swept away the old gods and the giants in one last battle with Loki and his evil power. Loki too was destroyed. The ramparts of Asgard fell, worlds crashed in ruin, and the universe was no more. But out of the chaos and dark night a new heaven and a new earth were born. In the sky, day dawned again, as bright as the smile of Balder the Beautiful.

In northern lands, winter still brings a long darkness. But when the sun seems to have gone forever and the mistletoe hangs on the bough, men remember Balder. Then they light their fires and live in the belief that Balder will come again.

Lewis's father gave him a gramophone. The Wagnerian music opened up the entire "Ring" music for him with the heroic drama of "The Ride of the Valkyries" giving new meaning to *The Twilight of the Gods."*

THE WATER BABIES—A FAIRY TALE FOR A LAND BABY
by CHARLES KINGSLEY

This book is in the Lewis library, inscribed "to Florence A. Hamilton from her father and mother on her birthday 1872." Flora would have been ten years old.

When Lewis was in his thirties, he told of reading Kingsley's *Water Babies*. The most incredibly faint memories began to come to him — feeling his mother's presence as he remembered her reading it to him, a very early memory. "She must have read it or started to read it when I was very young. I had even a curious sense of bringing my mother to life, as if she were reading it through me."[6]

"WATER BABIES"— ADAPTED.

"What have we done for God?"

—Flora Hamilton Lewis

THERE CAME A NIGHT

When he was ten, Lewis lost his mother to cancer. It was a great shock to this sensitive boy who felt that "all settled happiness" had gone. Flora had begun to teach him Latin and French and had taken the boys to northern France on one of their holidays. He had been educated at home by his governess, Annie Harper; now he would be sent to schools in England. Warren and Jack drew closer than ever to each other, feeling withdrawn from their grief-stricken father.

After ten years of marriage in August 1904, Flora Hamilton wrote, "I do not think that very many wives can feel as sure of their husband's love as I do after ten years, ten very happy, good years.

Your love still as fresh and warm as when you first loved me. I have every confidence that the coming ones will be as good."[1]

After her death, Albert wrote wistfully in an effort to achieve some equilibrium:

"When she who made our lives was here
To smooth the ruffled way
Hungry memory drives me like her
To work and love and pray.
To be like her — work, love and pray." [2]

Friends at her death spoke of her concerns for her family and of her goodness to her father-in-law, who lived with them. "What a mother," one commented.

The lovely summer holidays with their mother, Flora Hamilton Lewis, were at an end, though following her cancer surgery on February 15, 1908, Jacks and his mother went to Flora's sister-in-law's home at the little County Antrim port of Larne Harbor. It was a convalescent visit to the beloved Aunt Annie, the Canadian wife of Uncle Gussie. Lewis wrote from there, May 20, 1908, "Mamy is doing very well indeed,"

STAINED GLASS WINDOW GIVEN TO ST. MARKS CHURCH, DUNDELAY, BY C. S. LEWIS AND WARREN LEWIS.

AUNT ANNIE

Annie Hamilton (Aunt Annie), the Canadian wife of Flora's brother Augustus, was alike in friendship and temperament to their mother. She held a special place in their affections. She was very close to Flora and helped somewhat to assuage the emptiness after she had died.

Jack found her to be sensible and kindly without sentimentality. He also enjoyed "Uncle Gussie," her husband, who treated him as an equal.

Albert sent his sister-in-law to investigate the problems at Jack's school Wynyard. This formidable woman got the better of the difficult headmaster, and for a time conditions were better.

and so it seemed to his ten-year-old heart. He felt privileged to accompany his dear mother alone on this trip, as Warnie was in school in England.

But it was "the final bright flame from the dying candle," for Flora died three months later, August 23, 1908.

"There came a night" he wrote, "when I was ill and crying both with headache and toothache and distressed because my mother did not come to me."[3] Their mother had gradually been withdrawn from the boys into the hands of the nurses and doctors.

Flora had given each of her boys a Bible "from Mamy with fondest love, August 1908." The little gold-edged, black leather Bibles were her last gift to them. As she lay dying, her husband Albert spoke of God's great goodness to them. "What have we done for God?" she replied. In that hour, Flora Lewis could not have known the great blessings which her son Jacks would someday give to the world in his writings that showed his personal faith in the Lord Jesus Christ. She could only have imagined that her little son, who so adored the knights of the chessboard and knights in armor, would go forth to vanquish the giants of skepticism and to conquer the dragons of unbelief.

Could not Lewis's view of death have been greatly affected by the death of his mother when he was so young? In his correspondence he insisted that one should not try to pretend that death did not happen.

As a child he prayed for his mother's healing but commented later that he had approached God "without love, without awe, even without fear . . . almost as a magician with no religious importance."

In *The Magician's Nephew*, one of the Narnian Chronicles, there are echoes of his own wishful thinking as a child, as he tells of Digory, a boy in London who lived with his invalid mother. Digory was sent into the mountains of the western world where he was commissioned by Aslan to find an apple tree on a green hilltop in a garden and bring back a perfect apple. From its seed a new tree sprang up which protected Narnia from evil. Aslan gave Digory an apple from it to heal his mother. It cured her and he buried the core in his backyard. And from those seeds a tree grew up from which the wood was fashioned by Digory, much later, into a wardrobe, and that wardrobe retained some of its Narnian magic. The very natural conversations of Digory and his playmate Polly resemble Lewis's own childhood, for the time described makes them contemporaries.

11

SCHOOL DAYS

"In my

coracle of

verses

I will sing

of lands

unknown."

— C. S. Lewis

Less than a month after his mother's death, ten-year-old Jack was on his way to an English school with his brother Warren. Wynyard, referred to later in Lewis's writings as "Belsen," was located at Watford, Hertforshire, a very different terrain, flat and interminable, from his beloved Irish hills. They had crossed the Irish Sea by ship which separated him from everything he had known. His description of the clothes he now had to wear — a thick dark suit with Eton collar and knickerbockers that buttoned tightly at the knee with a firm-fitting bowler hat — contrasted sharply with the shorts and blazer and sand shoes that he had been running about in at home. In addition, the new heavy boots were most uncomfortable.

C. S. Lewis and his father.

The Bodleian Tower, Oxford.

Arriving at Wynyard, he was in awe and fear of the big, bearded man, "Oldie," the headmaster, and observed the well-used canes on the chimneypiece of the schoolroom. The students were made to do arithmetic sums endlessly, never a very good subject with him at best. "Oldie" taught geometry with a vengeance, forcing his students to reason. Albert Lewis had looked into many schools, and his choice of this school in its declining years, with a headmaster that was going insane, was most unfortunate.

The most important thing at that time to the boy Lewis was the effect on him of the Puritanism of his Ulster childhood contrasted with the very different Anglo-Catholic church to which he was required to go. He feared for his soul and began seriously to pray and to read his Bible. He enjoyed reading, at that time, the fiction about the ancient

CAMPBELL COLLEGE,
BELFAST, IRELAND.

world: *Quo Vadis, The Gladiators,* and *Ben Hur,* to name a few. He also read H. G. Wells' science fiction. School holidays were "longed for" with great hope. His father finally realized his mistake and enrolled Jack in Campbell College in 1910 — a public school in Ireland only a mile from Little Lea.

In January 1911, Lewis attended Cherbourg Preparatory School in Worcestershire, England. He liked the green plains and the green peaked hills and studied Latin and English. But a matron, who had a passion for the occult, blunted the edges of his belief in God. Here he abandoned his faith and developed a pessimism that led him to feel that the universe was a menacing and unfriendly place. In telling his story of these years in his autobiography, *Surprised by Joy,* he equated some of this with the strange awkwardness of his hands, feeling that everything would do what he did not want it to do. He admits that it sounds comic, but this resistance on the part of inanimate things, as he became a teenager, gave his mind an early bias. Knots did not stay tied. Straight things became bent. He felt that there would be terms and holidays and work until he died and recalled his father's often-voiced warning that one must somehow avoid the workhouse by extreme exertion.

A very sobering observation was that "most of those who think, have done their thinking in the first fourteen years."

Though in bed with a temperature, Lewis, in 1913, won a scholarship to Malvern. Here there came a reawakening of what he

had lost from his later childhood. It was the sense of his own past joy as he discovered "Northernness" in *Siegfried and the Twilight of the Gods*. He learned what writing means and delighted in the great operas and Wagner's music. "The Ride of the Valkyries" was heroic drama and seeing this in nature and in poetry as the "honey-tongued" teacher, Smewgy, turned the verses into music, was ecstasy.

All of this while enduring the class-conscious struggles of his classmates, many of whom were proud of their athletic prowess. He mistakenly got into the wrong club and found that with the forced duties toward older boys he could hardly keep up with his work. He was a big boy and had overgrown his strength. Much of the activity was boring to him, but having to pretend an interest was tiring.

The school library, "The Gurney," was, however, a sanctuary. To find books, silence, and leisure was freedom indeed. Here he discovered Celtic and Greek mythology as well as Milton and Yeats.

When Jacks was first away at school in England, he received a letter from his father on his birthday November 29, 1908, from Belfast:

"My dear Klicks,

From the bottom of my heart I wish you a happy birthday and I pray that the blessing of God Almighty may be upon you and Warnie all the days of your life. With warmest love to you both, ever your loving Paps."[1]

LETTERS OF ENCOURAGEMENT
TO JACK FROM HIS FATHER, SIGNED PAPS

2 June 1912

"I can't tell you how pleased I was to get your letter enclosing the 'stars.' Things like that are as good as tonic." [2]

20 October 1912

"But there is one other small matter in your letter which demands a word. Just imagine C. S. L. writing 'acceptable acquisition' and calling it a 'good phrase.' What a hideous combination of jarring sounds. 'Acc-ac-acc-ac,' why it reminds one of the croaking chorus from the Frogs of Aristophanes." [3]

4 November 1912

"These stars that are falling in clusters are very pleasant and cheering to see. . . . I am looking forward with confidence to a scholarship next year." [4]

And referring to their deceased mother: *"How good and loving she was to all of us. Never forget her. Dear, dear Mamy was everything to me."* [5]

And writing to Jack on his fourteenth birthday, *"The Lord bless you and keep you,"* he wrote, after asking, *"How are you off for warm underclothes?"* [6]

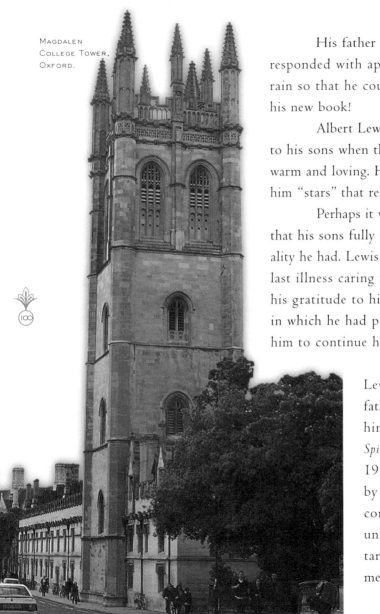

His father sent him the book *Joseph*, and Jack responded with appreciation, hoping that it would rain so that he could stay inside at school and read his new book!

Albert Lewis's concern, as shown in his letters to his sons when they were at school in England, was warm and loving. He encouraged Jack, who was sending him "stars" that represented excellent schoolwork.

Perhaps it was not until their father had died that his sons fully realized what a tremendous personality he had. Lewis spent some time during his father's last illness caring for him. He had often expressed his gratitude to his father over the years for the way in which he had provided and made it possible for him to continue his years of study at Oxford.

During his first year at Oxford, Lewis was pleased to be able to tell his father, who had so greatly encouraged him, of publishing his first book, *Spirits in Bondage, a Cycle of Lyrics*, in 1919. He acknowledged his Welshness by writing in the prologue, "In my coracle of verses I will sing of lands unknown." (The coracle is a small, tarred, single craft that salmon fishermen have used from early Roman days.)

The poems in *Spirits in Bondage* were written by the youthful Lewis from 1915 onwards, showing the influences of both Keats and Yeats. In *Daily Bread* he depicts a life of spiritual pilgrimage searching for "that gulf of light" in preexistence, years before he was converted.

Amazing, it seems, that this boy, destined to be such an exponent of Christian truth in the world, should have been sent back to the false gods in order to acquire "some capacity for worship against the day when the true God would recall him to Himself." [7]

Finally, in 1914, he was sent to William T. Kirkpatrick at Great Bookham, Surrey. "The Great Knock," as he was called by Lewis's father, had also helped Warren. A balding man, over six foot tall, lean and muscular with mustache and side whiskers, he spoke pure Ulster. Kirk was quite ruthless in begging to have statements clarified. He wanted to know if there was evidence for what one declared.

W.T. KIRKPATRICK AND HIS WIFE, 1920.

Lewis liked such conversations — ones rational and ones imaginative. He enjoyed the routine at Gastons, the Kirkpatrick's house. In the evenings he had French with Mrs. Kirkpatrick, while during the day there were Homer, Herodotus, Virgil, Euripides, Sophocles, and others. There were Greek and Latin compositions too.

About this time another "good" had occurred for Lewis. That was the friendship he discovered with his Irish neighbor, Arthur Greeves, three years older than he. They had much the same taste in books and reveled together in "The Myth of the Norsemen." To find that there do exist people very like oneself was a revelation to both. Their frequent letters to each other were a source of delight and information.

When C. S. Lewis was in school at Bookham, he liked to walk to Leatherhead and take the train back at dusk, where the smoke of an engine glowed red on the underside, reflecting the furnace.

On one of these trips he bought George Macdonald's book *Phantastes* at the station to read on the train. Crediting the experience to be one of crossing "a great frontier" and discovering the quality of goodness or holiness which, as he said, "baptized" his imagination.

"For the first time," he wrote, "the song of the sirens sounded like the voice of my mother or my nurse. I saw the bright shadow coming out of the book into the real world."[8] (Later Lewis said that *Phantastes* had filled for him the place of a devotional book.)

In Warnie's room at the Kilns, Doug Gresham (Lewis's stepson) later found, on the wall, a picture of the engine that pulled the Tal-y-Llyn (Wales) train. Warren Lewis had a small "share" in this railroad.

BLACKWELL'S BOOKS, OXFORD.

Jack and Warnie had always been infatuated with trains. While at Castlerock, he and his brother would get up early to watch them from their bedroom window.

Attending mainly English schools as a boy, Lewis went on to become a scholar at University College, Oxford, and later a don (or "fellow") of English at Magdalen, Oxford, and professor at Magdalene, Cambridge.

Lewis had been at University College in Oxford less than a term when his papers came through, and was drafted into a Cadet Battalion in Keble in 1917. He was commissioned as a second lieutenant in the Somerset Light Infantry. Later he was wounded and spent some time in the hospital. In January 1919, he was able to return to Oxford and resume his studies. "I call her my mother" Lewis wrote of Mrs. Moore who, with her daughter Maureen, lived with him. Her son Paddy had been a friend of Lewis's during the war, and they had agreed to look after each other's parents should one of them not survive. Paddy Moore was killed, and thereafter, until her death many years later, Lewis looked after his mother.

Moving into the Kilns in Headington Quarry, a suburb of Oxford, in 1933, Lewis experienced

MAGDALEN COLLEGE FROM ADDISON'S WALK.

JACK LEWIS WITH KEBLE COLLEGE CADET ROOMATE, E.F.C. ("PADDY") MOORE, IN A PUNT IN OXFORD, 1917.

WARNIE'S ROOM, LOWER RIGHT, AT THE KILNS.

the feeling, as a country householder, of now actually being "a part of England." About three miles from Oxford on a bus route, the house was on property where earlier two huge kilns had stood for the making of brick. The new place was at the foot of a large oak tree, down a long lane, and hidden by shrubs and small trees.

Lewis had rented other places, but the Kilns became his own home and the home of Mrs. Janie Moore; Maureen; Lewis's brother Warren; and Mr. Papworth, the dog. The occupants proceeded to make much-needed improvements. Outside, the brothers planted trees and cleared the property of weeds and brambles.

Nearby at the base of Shotover Hill, there was a pond known locally as Shelley's pool,[9] where clay had been removed for brick-making. It became a place for swimming and boating, with a punt, which Jack and Warren built.

The house was made hospitable for friends with Mrs. Moore cooking and housekeeping. During World War II, some children evacu-ated from London were cared for at the Kilns. It was a place that afforded Jack opportunity to read and write and enjoy country walks, though he often did "double duty" in the kitchen. To him the house had "a good night feeling." He stayed in his rooms at Magdalen most of the week, spending weekends at the Kilns. When later at Cambridge, he would return to his home by train, using the time to read and pray.

All kinds of weather to Jack were good. He liked the rain and storms and enjoyed winter days. He wrote of the flowers and the tiny snowdrops near the Kilns, which heralded spring. C. S. Lewis believed that God has shared with us the secrets of nature, and they are associated with the important doctrine of the resurrection of the body.

WALKING COUNTRY NEAR SHOTOVER HILL (SOUTH OF THE KILNS).

12

SOMETHING OTHER

DEER PARK GATE AT ADDISON'S WALK

G. K. Chesterton's book *The Everlasting Man* seemed to make sense to Lewis as he struggled against a belief in Christianity. And then in 1926, he was alarmed when a hard-boiled atheist sat in his room on the other side of the fire and remarked that there was evidence for the historicity of the Gospels. "Rum thing," he said, "about the dying God. Rum thing. It almost looks as if it had really happened once."

Two years later Lewis told of strolling along Addison's walk on a blustery night with his friends J. R. R. Tolkien and Hugh Dyson. They discussed the purpose of myth and of "true mythology." They talked in Lewis's rooms until three in the morning. Then Lewis and Dyson walked up and down the cloisters of new buildings

C. S Lewis and Warren.

Magdalen College,
C. S. Lewis's room,
2nd floor, far right.

"Sometimes I can almost think that I was sent back to the false gods there to acquire some capacity for worship against the day when the true God should recall me to Himself."[1]

— C.S. Lewis

107

at Magdalen, talking until the sky grew light. Later Lewis was to acknowledge that Dyson and Tolkien were the immediate human causes of his conversion.

His description of his conversion in *Surprised by Joy*, his autobiography, leaves some puzzled. What did it mean? "I was driven (in Warren's sidecar) to Whipsnade Zoo one sunny morning. When we set out I did not believe that Jesus Christ is the Son of God, and when we reached the zoo, I did." Lewis tells of this as the last step. "Every step I had taken" he wrote, "from the Absolute to 'Spirit' and from 'Spirit' to 'God' had been a step toward the more imminent, the more compulsive."[2] He knew now that all "his waitings and watching for Joy were merely the mental track left by the passage of Joy." That Joy had been "a pointer to something other and outer," which he had now found.

After his conversion he found skies bluer and grass greener. "Today" he wrote to Arthur, "I got such a sudden intense feeling of delight that it sort of stopped me in my walk and spun me round. Indeed the sweetness was so great, and seemed so to affect the whole body as well as the mind, that it gave me pause. . . . Everything seems . . . to be beginning again and one has the sense of immortality. . . . I really seem to have had youth given back to me lately."[3]

PUNTS ALONG THE CHERWLL RIVER.

THE DAY WITH A WHITE MARK

by C. S. LEWIS

All day I have been tossed and
whirled in a preposterous happiness:

Was it an elf in the blood? Or a
bird in the brain? Or even part

Of the cloudily crested, fifty-league-
long, loud uplifted wave

Of a journeying angel's transit
roaring over and through my heart?

My garden's spoiled, my holidays are
cancelled, the omens harden;

The plann'd and unplann'd miseries
deepen; the knots draw tight.

Reason kept telling me all day my
mood was out of season.

It was, too. In the dark ahead the
breakers only are white.

Yet I — I could have kissed the very
scullery taps. The colour of

My day was like a peacock's chest.
In at each sense there stole

Ripplings and dewy sprinkles of
delight that with them drew

Fine threads of memory through the
vibrant thickness of the soul.

As though there were transparent earths
and luminous trees should grow there,

And shining roots worked visibly far
down below one's feet,

So everything, the tick of the clock,
the cock crowing in the yard

Probing my soul, woke diverse buried
hearts of mine to beat,

Recalling either adolescent heights
and the inaccessible

Longings and ice-sharp joys that
shook my body and turned me pale,

Or humbler pleasures, chuckling as
it were in the ear, mumbling

Of glee, as kindly animals talk in
a children's tale.

Who knows if ever it will come again,
now the day closes?

No one can give me, or take away,
that key. All depends

On the elf, the bird, or the angel.
I doubt if the angel himself

Is free to choose when sudden heaven
in man begins or ends.[4]

13

I WROTE THE BOOKS...

"I wrote the books I should have liked to read... That's always been my reason for writing."[1]

— C. S. Lewis

It is difficult to choose portions from the rich feast spread out in C. S. Lewis's prolific writings. Included here are a few favorites which can only whet one's appetite to read some of the forty books he wrote before his death in 1963. Since then the number has expanded to sixty-eight because of hitherto unpublished manuscripts that have now been published, as well as books featuring his letters.

Though Lewis was never accused of copying another author, there are, however, subconscious overtones in Lewis's books that emphasize some of the things that delighted him as a child. He was quick to point out those to whom he was indebted. He believed that his fairy tales and science-fiction stories of space aroused longing for more ideal worlds. Myth was not falsehood.

CENTENARY STATUE OF C.S. LEWIS IN DUNDELA (BELFAST), IRELAND.

BOOKS WRITTEN BY C.S. LEWIS.

In his stories he featured animals that could talk, fauns, satyrs, centaurs, and dragons. There were doors that one could go through by magic; floating islands that one could rest on.

And above all, there was Aslan, the lion, who said to the girl Jill, "You would not have called to me, unless I had been calling you."

In describing his writing of the *Narnian Chronicles* "in the tradition of E. Nesbit," Lewis asserts that Aslan (Turkish for lion) came "bounding in." Aslan is the figure of Christ around which these stories revolve.

"I wrote the books I should have liked to read if I could have got them. That's always been my reason for writing. People don't write the books I want so I have to do it for myself: no rot about 'self expression.'"[2]

THE SEARCHER
- CENTENARY STATUE BY MR. ROSS WILSON

The bronze statue stands in front of Holywood Road Branch Library, Belfast, Ireland, a short distance from Little Lea. It was unveiled on the 100th anniversary of C. S. Lewis's birth, November 1998.

The inscription on the walk surrounding the statue reads:

C. S. 'JACK' LEWIS-ULSTERMAN
WRITER, SCHOLAR, TEACHER, CHRISTIAN
BORN 1898, REBORN 1931
THE SEARCHER CENTENARY SCULPTURE

THE SEARCHER

The searcher is based on a literary character called Digory Kirke created by C. S. Lewis. In *The Magician's Nephew* it was Digory who made the wardrobe from a beautiful apple tree that had magical properties, which helped open a doorway to Narnia and Aslan.

WARDROBES

C. S. Lewis did not just hang clothes in a wardrobe, he hung ideas — great ideas of sacrifice, redemption, victory and freedom for the sons of Adam and the daughters of Eve — set within the commonplace, revelation within something that looks ordinary on the outside — revelation through investigation. We should not stop looking, some of the greatest things can be found in the most ordinary of places, like a wardrobe. - RW 1998

"This is precisely what Christianity is about. This world is a great sculptor's shop. We are the statues and there is a rumor going round the shop that some of us are someday going to come to life." - C. S. LEWIS

INSCRIPTION ON THE BACK OF
THE BRONZE WARDROBE STATUE.

CAST BRONZE FOUNDRY DUBLIN

The Narnian books were always among his favorites, and he particularly enjoyed the great number of letters of appreciation which children wrote to him about them. Most of all he was gratified by the fact that children never seemed in doubt as to the identity of Aslan — while many grown-ups completely missed it.

One finds again and again in C. S. Lewis's writings echoes from the Bible, from literature, from legend. There is the binding of Gulliver, Arthur's mystic round table and stone knife. He speaks of "The Stable," in *The Last Battle*, "that once had something inside that was bigger than our whole world."[3] There are gentle giants in *The Silver Chair* and dwarves of the underworld in the *Waste Lands of the North* — good triumphing over the evil forces that seek control.

The world of Lewis's boyhood had much in common with Kipling, and for Kipling he had great admiration.

C. S. Lewis's childhood would seem unusual nowadays and would indeed be almost impossible, however ordinary it was a century ago. "In those days Mr. Sherlock Holmes was still living in Baker Street and the Bastables were looking for treasure in Lewisham Road,"[4] as he wrote of *The Magician's Nephew*. If sometimes the children in the Narnian stories speak a little oddly, or seem to be imitating E. Nesbit's children, one must remember that Lewis was himself a child when Nesbit was writing — and he is not borrowing from her.

Just a few weeks before his death, C. S. Lewis wrote the following letter. It seems almost inspired.

Dear Ruth Broady,

Many thanks for your kind letter, and it was very good of you to write and tell me that you like my books; and what a very good letter you write for your age!

If you continue to love Jesus, nothing much can go wrong with you, and I hope you may always do so. I'm so thankful that you realized the "hidden story" in the Narnian books. It is odd, children nearly always do, grownups hardly ever.

I'm afraid the Narnian series has come to an end, and am sorry to tell you that you can expect no more.

God bless you.

Yours sincerely,
C. S. Lewis

The Wardrobe was hand-carved of black bog oak by Jacksie's Grandfather Lewis. It stood for many years at Little Lea. Ruth Parker, Lewis's cousin, tells of sitting in this wardrobe while young Jack told stories. It was purchased at auction in England for Wheaton College, where it now stands in The Wade Center.

The children come by the dozens to look at the Wardrobe. Having read *The Lion, the Witch and the Wardrobe*, they are awed to see it. Opening the door they imagine it as the entrance into the Land of Narnia, wishing that, like the children in the story they could also enter there.

Lewis's first popular theological book, *The Screwtape Letters*, shows many reflections portraying the forces of evil and hell arrayed against the more powerful forces of good and of heaven. He entrusted his manuscript to Sister Penelope in Wantage, Ireland, during the war, "in case the publisher got blitzed."[6]

C. S. Lewis had written to Sister Penelope in Wantage, Ireland, in the '30s. She was the author of several books he admired. To her he mailed a copy of *The Screwtape Letters* and told her later (after the safekeeping was no longer required) to dispose of it as she saw fit. She sold the manuscript to the New York Public

Library when the convent needed money. Her original letters and correspondence from C. S. Lewis are in the Bodleian at Oxford.

Although Lewis wrote books of literary history and criticism at Oxford and Cambridge, it is religious studies such as *The Abolition of Man, The Problem of Pain, Miracles, The Four Loves, Mere Christianity,* and *Reflections on the Psalms* which provide us with the force of Christian ideas. In these studies, as well as in essays like "Christian Reflections," he makes Christianity compelling and convincing. Even in his religious fiction, *The Great Divorce, The Screwtape Letters,* and *The Pilgrim's Regress,* he writes of this "higher realism." That joy is "the serious business of heaven" is made quite clear. That one may find this joy on earth is shown as well.

Lewis's imagination and faith merged in his unique space trilogy: *Out of the Silent Planet, Perelandra,* and *That Hideous Strength.* In *Perelandra* (his favorite of the three) there is the supposition of a planet untouched by evil, like the original Garden of Eden. Dr. Elwin Ransom, the main character, is symbolically named. Writing in the '40s about the moon and early

JOY

by C. S. LEWIS

Today was all unlike another day.
    The long waves of my sleep near morning broke
    On happier beaches, tumbling lighted spray
    Of soft dreams filled with promise. As I woke,
    Like a huge bird Joy with the feathery stroke
    Of strange wings brushed me over. Sweeter air
    Came never from dawn's heart. The misty smoke
    Cooled it upon the hills. It touched the lair
    Of each wild thing and woke the wet flowers everywhere.[7]

(117)

THE NATIVITY

by C. S. LEWIS

Among the oxen (like an ox I'm slow)
I see a glory in the stable grow
Which, with the ox's dullness might at length
Give me an ox's strength.

Among the asses (stubborn I as they)
I see my Saviour where I looked for hay;

So may my beastlike folly learn at least
The patience of a beast.

Among the sheep (I like a sheep have strayed)
I watch the manger where my Lord is laid;
Oh that my baa-ing nature would win thence
Some woolly innocence![8]

rumors of actual travel in space, Lewis said, "I begin to be afraid that the villains will really contaminate the moon." His conception of outer space was an "expansion of experience." He felt it to be full rather than empty. The "earths," or planets, he saw as mere gaps in the living heaven, "formed not by addition to, but by subtraction from the surrounding brightness [the heavens]." The silent planet is our earth, the one to reject Heaven's Song.

"Till We Have Faces" is the story that C. S. Lewis liked best of his fiction writings. It is the telling of a myth within a myth — the meanings are difficult and require study. It is evident that the fiction is more true than fact. And one remembers that Lewis wrote these books because they were the kind which he, in fact, would like to have read. He wrote them because no one else had written them!

Mary Willis Shelburne sent Lewis one of her poems in 1953. "Yours is the better poem," he wrote, "but one must send the ball back over the net somehow."

His response to her was to write the "The Nativity."

14

THE HAPPIEST THREE YEARS

"I never expected to have in my sixties, the happiness that passed me by in my twenties." [1]

— C. S. Lewis

The interesting details which are revealed in his letters (letters which he never dreamed would be collected and published) show a most amazing dedication to duty. He did not like to write letters — "the pen has become to me like the oar to a galley slave." He wrote everything in long hand and often apologized for his "awful hand" due in part to a bone disease (osteoporosis), which made writing difficult and painful. Yet he rose early to answer his voluminous mail, believing it a part of his Christian duty to share his concern, advice, prayer, and even money with those in need. Thus we have such a correspondence as "Letters to an American Lady," written to help one in need of spiritual encouragement.

Lewis continued to write to the American lady, Mary Willis Shelburne, and said, "You are one of the minority of my numerous female correspondents who didn't gradually fade away as soon as they heard I was married."

A bachelor until the age of fifty-nine, Lewis married Joy Davidman Gresham in 1957. She was an American

JOY DAVIDMAN LEWIS.

JOY DAVIDMAN'S HOME IN HEADINGTON (PRIOR TO MARRYING C.S. LEWIS).

of Jewish heritage, whom he had known a long time. Their romance is touching and poignant.

Joy had been converted to Christianity largely through reading Lewis's books. He married her at a hospital bedside because of her illness (cancer). "The fact that she was facing pain and death and anxiety about the future of her children" (two sons, David and Douglas, by her first husband) was "an extra reason." Because of his love and concern for her as she was facing death, they were later married in a religious ceremony. The disease was arrested, and they had what Lewis described as "the happiest three years of my life." He wrote of her death and his sorrow in *A Grief Observed*, using the pen name N. W. Clerk. He who had sought so persistently for joy, who had such a profound sense of "longing," had been granted an earthly "Joy."

Joy's son Douglas once found them weeping together while reading the poetry of John Keats.

SIX BELLS PUB NEAR THE KILNS.

In April 1960 they travelled by air to Greece. Joy climbed with her husband Jack to the top of the Acropolis, and they got as far as the Lion gate of Mycenae, "absolutely enraptured" by all they saw. But she died in July, and his grief was "like a winding road with quite a new landscape at each bend."[2]

Some time after Joy's death, Jack composed a brief verse in her memory. It was inscribed on an austere marble plaque shaped like a crucifix and mounted on a memorial wall in the crematorium garden. The inscription reads:

R EMEMBER
H ELEN J OY
D AVIDMAN
D. J ULY 1960
L OVED WIFE OF
C. S. L EWIS

Here the whole world (stars, water, air,
And field, and forest, as they were
Reflected in a single mind)
Like cast off clothes was left behind

In ashes yet with hope that she,
Re-born from holy poverty,
In lenten lands, hereafter may
Resume them on her Easter Day.[3]

A GRIEF SHARED

" My

younger

stepson

is the

greatest

comfort

to me." 1

— C. S. Lewis

As I went up to the locked door of the Wade Collection room on that Saturday morning in May 1983, I seemed to have difficulty getting the key to turn.

"Here, let me help you, I've opened a lot of doors with or without a key." I supposed he was a "researcher," this good-looking young man wearing pale, off-white, trousers and calf length leather boots.

When the door was opened, he drew himself up to his full height and said, "I am C. S. Lewis's stepson, Douglas Gresham." We entered the quite book-lined room, and the wardrobe was the first thing he saw. "Oh," he exclaimed, going to the wardrobe, reaching up, and unlatching the left-hand door. (Everyone used the right-hand door, not knowing about the latch.)

C.S. Lewis with David
(left) and Douglas Gresham
at The Kilns, 1957.

125

"Did you see that?" he said, almost as a way of proving who he was! The door of the beautiful hand-carved wardrobe made by Lewis's grandfather was now open. "This is Warnie's coat," he said, fumbling in the pocket. "He usually had bus tickets in his pocket. I kept my rain things in this wardrobe."

Doug sat at the big table in the reading room. "This was our dining room table." I showed him a copy of *Letters to an American Lady.* "Have you ever seen this?" Lewis had written that Doug was such a comfort to him in the loss of Joy. "Why would I be a comfort to him?" he asked.

After C. S. Lewis and Joy's marraige, Doug and his brother David had come with their mother to live at the Kilns. Lewis supplied funds for the boys' schooling, as he had done a number of children.[2] Doug told of "Cobbler," the pony, that Lewis had bought for him.

In the days that followed at The Wade Center, Doug poured over the many books and letters. We had the privilege of entertaining him and his sweet wife, Merrie, and their four children, who, at that time, had been living in Australia.

Their home is in Ireland now, and the lad who, at age eleven, came to live at the home of Jack and Warnie has made it his responsibility to help establish the C. S. Lewis heritage. His 1988 book, *Lenten Lands,* gives us a picture of what it was like to be a child there at the Kilns.[3] His deep regard and love for both C. S. Lewis and his brother, Warnie, is very evident.

Perhaps because Lewis had lost his mother at a young age, he could sympathize deeply with Doug in his sorrow over his mother's death.

The Kilns, Headington Quarry, Oxford, England.[4]

127

16

CHAUCER'S KNIGHT

"And thou were the goodliest person that ever came among press of knights. And thou were the kindest man that ever struck with sword."1

—Sir Thomas Malory

*T*he Oxford History of English Literature, Volume III was Lewis's most onerous academic labor. It was ten years in the writing, and he longed to finish it so that he could get on with what he considered "really worthwhile" — theology and fantasy. "The book exemplifies Lewis's gift for summing up the virtues of a work," wrote Dame Helen Gardner of the British Academy, a tutor at Oxford. "The book is brilliantly written, compulsively readable and constantly illuminated by sentences that are as true as they are witty. Who else could have written a literary history that continually arouses delighted laughter! There is hardly a page that does not stimulate and provoke thought."2

PARISH CHURCH AND
C.S. LEWIS' GRAVE,
HEADINGTON QUARRY,
ENGLAND.

129

IN LOVING MEMORY OF
MY BROTHER
CLIVE STAPLES LEWIS
BORN BELFAST 29TH NOVEMBER 1898

In this same British Academy obituary, Dame Helen Gardner wrote after C. S. Lewis's death on November 22, 1963: "He gave an impression of a resolute cheerfulness and equanimity — an extremely powerful and original personality. He aroused warm affections, loyalty and devotion in his friends and feelings of almost equal strength among innumerable persons who knew him only through his books."[3] She admits that there was disapproval and distaste among some of his colleagues who did not like his books of Christian faith. And from an editorial in *The Cambridge Review*, "It is Chaucer's Knight, rather than his Parson, who comes most often to mind when one remembers C. S. Lewis. He was a chivalric figure and his imagination ran most richly in the forms of chivalry and adventure. Epic and romance were his great loves."[4]

"How little people know who think that holiness is dull," Lewis wrote. "When one meets the real thing it is irresistible." He could relate to others who were searching because of his own torturous journey from childhood faith into atheism, back to theism and finally to Jesus, the Son of God. Reflecting on Paul's epistles, he expressed amazement at the magnitude of the incarnation: the sacrifice of "the dying God." "It really happened," he declared.

Private prayer became very important to him, and of all sins he felt that pride was probably the deadliest.

Lewis did not believe that the world through progress was getting better and better. He did believe in the devil's continuous influence in the world. But he believed in the full revelation of God in Jesus, the ultimate victor King, whose glory and power cannot be conquered.

"We live in fact, in a world starved for solitude, silence and privacy and therefore starved for meditation and true friendship."[5] Although Lewis never came to America, he was pleased that his books were read here with such enthusiasm. His letters also showed a zest for life which he was careful not to suppress.

In one of his letters, he told what he would like to see in America after coming on a slow cargo boat! He mentioned three or four good friends and after New England, the "Rip Van Winkle" Mountains, Nantucket, and Huckleberry Finn country. A sub-Arctic winter appealed to him as well as the sight of a bear, a real forest, and a snowshoe.

In August 1951, Lewis told of revisiting Castlerock with his brother, where they had spent so many happy holidays with their mother. He spoke of surf-bathing again in the icy, self-foaming waters; walking again on the "firm, gently shivering sand;" looking for the history of the Bruces in the ancient cemetery there; of falling asleep to the murmur of the sea outside their windows, and feeling drugged by it.[6]

Years later, at his home the Kilns, Lewis wrote at his mother's desk, which he remembered having been in the drawing room at Little Lea. And he wondered "when last it was written at."

> "We search the world for truth
> And come back weary with our quest
> To find that all the sages said
> Was in the Book our mother read."
>
> (author unknown)

"Now indeed mountains and seas divide us; God grant on that Day hereafter, Day of resurrection of the body, yes, and of all things made, beyond our telling now — God grant us on that Day to meet!"[7]

The Latin Letters translated by Martin Moynihan

In the last chapter of *The Last Battle*, the seventh book of *The Chronicles of Narnia*, C. S. Lewis gives a parallel to his own nostalgic and distant memory of the lovely childhood holidays with his mother and brother in the north of Ireland.

The children in the story wonder where this beautiful land is. They see the sky and smell the morning freshness in the air.

"Peter," said Lucy, "where is this, do you suppose?"

"I don't know," said Peter, "but it reminds me of somewhere, but I can't give it a name. Could it be somewhere we once stayed for a holiday when we were very, very young?" Lucy declared that it was different than she remembered and "more . . . more." The children concluded that the earlier place was a shadow or copy of the real thing — as different as "waking life is from a dream." For them this was the beginning of the real story. "Come farther up and farther in," they were invited.

As a young man, C. S. Lewis wrote in his book *Spirits in Bondage*:

"SEEKING THE LAST STEEP EDGES
WHENCE I MAY LEAP INTO THAT GULF OF LIGHT."

In his writings, that have blessed so many, we know that he experienced those "steep edges." We also believe that later he was triumphantly welcomed into the glorious light of heaven.

PREFACE

1. John Milton, *Paradise Regained, Book IV.*

2. C. S. Lewis, *Surprised by Joy: The Shape of My Early Life* (London: Bles 1955), 5

3. Major Warren Lewis willed the *Lewis Papers* to the Marion E. Wade Center at Wheaton College.

4. C. S. Lewis, *Mere Christianity* (New York: Collins Fontana Books, 1952), back cover.

5. C. S. Lewis, *The Problem of Pain* (London: Geoffrey Bles Centenary Press, 1962 [1940]), the French edition.

INTRODUCTION

1. Lewis, *Surprised by Joy,* 183.

2. Clarence Benson, *A Guide for Child Study* (Chicago: Evangelical Teacher Training Association, 1950), 8.

CHAPTER ONE:
Little Lad Chattering

1. Milton, Book IV, line 220.

CHAPTER TWO:
We Built the Promenade

1. Leo Baker, contemporary Oxford friend of C. S. Lewis, *C. S. Lewis at the Breakfast Table,* ed. James T. Como (New York: Collier Books, Macmillan Publishers, 1979), 9.

2. C. S. Lewis, flyleaf inscription to his father, Albert, *Spirits in Bondage – A Cycle of Lyrics* (Heinemann, 1919).

3. Warren Hamilton Lewis, *"C. S. Lewis: A Biography,"* unpublished typescript in The Marion E. Wade Collection, Wheaton College, Wheaton, Illinois.

CHAPTER THREE:
Mamy Is Like . . .

1. *"The Lewis Papers: Memoirs of the Lewis Family, 1850-1930,"* vol. II (Leeborough Press), assembled by Albert Lewis, edited and typed by Warren Lewis, a typescript of the original is in The Marion E. Wade Collection, Wheaton College, Wheaton, Illinois, Flora Hamilton to Albert, June 26, 1893.

2. Walter Hooper, *C. S. Lewis Companion and Guide,* 6. As written by C. S. Lewis, age 9, in his Diary, 1907.

3. *"The Lewis Papers,"* Flora Hamilton to Albert, 18 August 1893.

4. Lewis, *Surprised by Joy,* 5.

CHAPTER FOUR:
I am Like Papy

1. C. S. Lewis diary, 1907.

2. Lewis, *Surprised by Joy,* 4.

CHAPTER FIVE:
Flora's Letters

1. Clarence Benson, *A Guide for Child Study* (Chicago: Evangelical Teaching Training Association, 1950), 19.

2. Lewis, *Surprised by Joy,* 5.

3. Grandfather Lewis who lived with them and Grandmother Hamilton who lived nearby.

4. Ibid., 12.

5. C. S. Lewis, *Letters to an American Lady,* ed. Clyde S. Kilby (Grand Rapids, Mich.: William B. Eerdman's Publishing Co., 1967), 23.

6. Lewis, *Surprised by Joy: The New Look,* 211.

7. Ibid., 216.

CHAPTER SIX:
It Was the First Beauty

1. Lewis, *Surprised by Joy,* 7.

2. George Sayer, *Jack* (Wheaton Ill.: Crossway Books, 1988), 52.

3. Lewis, *Surprised by Joy,* 10.

CHAPTER SEVEN:
My Brother's Gifts

1. Warren Lewis, *"The Lewis Papers."*

2. Lewis, *Surprised by Joy,* 10.

3. Ibid.

4. Warren Lewis, *"The Lewis Papers."*

5. C. S. Lewis, *"The Old Gray Mare"* poem permission from Elizabeth Stevens and Curtis Brown (Lewis Estate), *"The Lewis Papers,"* vol. II.

CHAPTER EIGHT:
Growing Up

1. George Sayer, *Jack,* 21.

2. *"The Lewis Papers."*

3. *"The Lewis Papers,"* Grandfather Lewis and nine-year-old Jacksie.

4. Lewis, *Surprised by Joy.*

CHAPTER NINE:
Books that Pleased

1. Lewis, *Surprised by Joy: The First Years,* 15.

2. E. Nesbit, *The Enchanted Castle.*

3. C. S. Lewis, *The Lion, the Witch and the Wardrobe* (London: Penguin Books, Geoffrey Bles, 1950), 150.

4. C. S. Lewis, *They Asked for a Paper* (London: Geoffrey Bles, 1962), chap. 2.

5. Lewis, *Surprised by Joy,* 231.

6. C. S. Lewis, *"The Letters of C. S. Lewis to Arthur Greeves,"* in *They Stand Together,* ed.

Walter Hooper (Macmillan Publishing Co.), letter dated 7 June 1930, 357. Used by permission from Elizabeth Stevens and Curtis Brown (Lewis Estate).

CHAPTER TEN:
There Came a Night

1. *"The Lewis Papers," vol. II,* Flora Hamilton to Albert.
2. Albert Lewis, *"The Lewis Papers,"* poem about his wife.
3. Lewis, *Surprised by Joy,* 18.

CHAPTER ELEVEN:
School Days

1. *"The Lewis Papers,"* letter to C. S. Lewis from his father, dated November 29, 1908.
2. Ibid., vol. III, Albert Lewis letter, 298.
3. Ibid., Albert Lewis letter, 298.
4. Ibid., Albert Lewis letter, 301.
5. Ibid., letter to Jack at school, dated 20 September 1908.
6. Ibid., Albert Lewis to Jack, dated 29 November 1912.
7. Lewis, *Surprised by Joy,* 77.
8. Ibid., 179.
9. Roger Lancelyn Green and Walter Hooper, *C. S. Lewis: A Biography,* p. 100. There is a tradition that Shelley used to meditate at the pond.

CHAPTER TWELVE:
Something Other

1. Lewis, *Surprised by Joy,* 79.
2. Ibid., 237.
3. C. S. Lewis, *They Stand Together,* used by permission of Lewis estate.
4. C. S. Lewis, *"The Day with a White Mark,"* ed. Walter Hooper, dated August 17, 1949 (London: Geoffrey Bles), 28-29.

CHAPTER THIRTEEN:
I Wrote the Books

1. C. S. Lewis, letter to a publisher, Chad Walsh, in *C. S. Lewis Apostle to the Skeptics* (New York: Macmillan, 1949), on dust jacket.
2. C. S. Lewis, *The Silver Chair* (London: Geoffrey Bles, 1953), 28.
3. C. S. Lewis, *The Last Battle* (Harmondsworth, England: Penguin Books, The Bodley Head, 1956), 128.
4. C. S. Lewis, *The Magician's Nephew* (Harmondsworth, England: Penguin Books, The Bodley Head, 1955), 9.
5. C. S. Lewis, *Letter to Ruth Broady,* dated 26 October 1963, *Letters to Children,* ed. Lyle Dorsett (New York: Macmillan Publishing Co., 1985), 111.
6. C. S. Lewis, *Letters to C. S. Lewis,* ed. W. H. Lewis (New York: Harcourt, Brace & World, Inc., 1966), letter to Sister Penelope, dated 9 October 1941.

7. C. S. Lewis poem *"Joy,"* dated April 1924 (originally published in *"The Beacon"*), *C. S. Lewis: A Biography* (London: Green and Hooper), 77. Used by permission of Elizabeth Stevens and Curtis Brown (Lewis estate).

8. C. S. Lewis, *"The Nativity,"* original poem given by Mary Willis Shelbourne to The Wade Center, C. S. Lewis Poems, ed. Walter Hooper (London: Geoffrey Bles, 1964), 122.

CHAPTER FOURTEEN:
The Happiest Three Years

1. Jocelyn Gibb, ed., *Light on C. S. Lewis* (HarperCollins, Geoffrey Bles, 1965), 43. As said to Nevill Coghill.

2. N. W. (Nat Whilk) Clerk, pseudonym for C. S. Lewis, *A Grief Observed* (London: Bantam, Faber and Faber, 1969; reprint. New York: The Seabury Press, Inc., 1963), 69.

3. Poem by C. S. Lewis in memory of his wife Joy Davidman Lewis inscribed on a marble plaque on The Memorial Wall in the crematorium garden.

CHAPTER FIFTEEN:
A Grief Shared

1. Lewis, *Letters to an American Lady*, 89.

2. C. S. Lewis had a secret charity fund that helped with the education of not only his stepsons, but many children. It was named Agaparg, personified as an imaginary giant of kindly disposition.

3. Douglas Gresham, *Lenten Lands.*

4. The Kilns has recently been restored by the C. S. Lewis Foundation. For more information on The Kilns and C. S. Lewis Foundation conferences contact: C. S. Lewis Foundation, P.O. Box 8008, Redlands, CA 92375.

CHAPTER SIXTEEN:
Chaucer's Knight

1. Sir Thomas Malory, *Le Morte d'Arthur.*

2. Dame Helen Gardner, Obituary of C. S. Lewis in British Academy, *The Proceedings, vol. LI* (London: Oxford University Press).

3. Ibid.

4. In Memoriam-The Cambridge Review.

5. Walter Hooper, ed., *They Stand Together* (Macmillan Publishing Co. Inc.). Used by permission of Elizabeth and Curtis Brown (Lewis estate).

6. Ibid.

7. C. S. Lewis, *The Latin Letters of C. S. Lewis*, trans. Martin Moynihan (Wheaton, Ill.: Crossway Books), 48. Written by C. S. Lewis, January 1949, from Magdalen College, Oxford, to Don Giovanni Calabria, an Italian priest.

BIBLIOGRAPHY

Benson, Clarence H. *A Guide for Child Study.* Chicago: Evangelical Teacher Training Assoc., 1950.

"Book of the Road." Reader's Digest, with The Automobile Association. London: Fanum House, 1967.

Clerk, N. W. (pseud.) *A Grief Observed.* London: Faber and Faber, 1961. Greenwich, Conn.: Seabury Press, 1963.

Como, James T., ed. *C. S. Lewis at the Breakfast Table.* New York: Collier Books, Macmillan Publishing Co. Revised and enlarged by Walter Hooper, includes a complete "Bibliography of the writings of C. S. Lewis" U. S.: Harcourt, Brace & World, Inc., 1979.

Doyle, Sir Arthur Conan. *Sir Nigel.* 1906.

Gibb, Jocelyn, ed. *Light on C. S. Lewis.* London: Geoffrey Bles, 1965. HarperCollins.

Green, Roger Lancelyn, and Walter Hooper. *C. S. Lewis, a Biography.* Williams Collins Sons & Co., Ltd. US: Harcourt, Brace & World, Inc. Can.: Souvenir Press, 1974.

Gresham, Douglas. *Lenten Lands,* Macmillan, 1988. William Collins Sons & Co., Ltd., 1989.

Hodges, Margaret. *Balder and the Mistletoe.*

Hooper, Walter. *C. S. Lewis Companion and Guide.* San Francisco: Harper, 1996.

Hooper, Walter, ed. *Poems.* San Diego: Harcourt Brace & Co., 1964.

Hooper, Walter, ed. *They Stand Together, The Letters of C. S. Lewis to Arthur Greeves (1914-1963).* Macmillan Publishing Co., Inc., 1979.

Huber, Miriam Blanton, ed. *Story and Verse for Children.* The Macmillan Co., 1955. ("Sigurd the Volsung," adapted from William Morris, 1876.)

Kilby, Clyde S. *The Christian World of C. S. Lewis.* Grand Rapids, Mich.: William B. Eerdman's Publishing Co., 1964.

Kilby, Clyde S., and Douglas Gilbert. *C. S. Lewis: Images of His World.* Grand Rapids, Mich.: William B. Eerdman's Publishing Co., 1973.

Kilby, Clyde S., and Marjorie Lamp Mead, eds. *Brothers and Friends, The Diaries of Warren Hamilton Lewis.* US, UK, Can.: HarperCollins US, 1982.

Kingsley, Rev. Charles. *The Water Babies.* 1863.

Lewis, C. S. *Complete Chronicles of Narnia.* US, UK, Can.: HarperCollins UK, 1995.

Lewis, C. S. *Letters to an American Lady.* Ed. Clyde S. Kilby. Grand Rapids, Mich.: William B. Eerdman's Publishing Co., 1967.

Lewis, C. S. *Mere Christianity.* Collins, Fontana Books. US, UK, Can.: HarperCollins UK, 1952.

Lewis, C. S. *Of Other Worlds.* US: Harcourt, Brace & World, Inc. UK, Can.: HarperCollins UK, 1966.

Lewis, C. S. *Problem of Pain.* London: Geoffrey Bles Centenary Press, 1940.

Lewis, C. S. *The Screwtape Letters.* Macmillan Publishing Co., Inc. US, UK, Can.: HarperCollins UK, 1942.

Lewis, C. S. *Spirits in Bondage, a Cycle of Lyrics.* London: William Heinemann. US: Harcourt, Brace & World, Inc. HarperCollins UK, 1919.

Lewis, C. S. *Surprised by Joy, the Shape of My Early Life.* Harcourt, Brace & World, Inc. HarperCollins UK, 1955.

Lewis, C. S. *They Asked for a Paper.* London: Geoffrey Bles, 1962.

Lewis, C. S. *The Weight of Glory.* Sermon at Christ Church, Oxford, 8 June 1941.

Lewis, C. S., and Geoffrey Bles. *Letters to Malcolm, Chiefly on Prayer.* London: Harcourt, Brace & World, Inc. US: Harcourt, Brace & World, Inc. UK, Can.: HarperCollins UK, 1964.

Lewis, Warren H., ed., *Letters of C. S. Lewis,* Harcourt, Brace & World, Inc., 1966.

Lewis, Warren H., ed. *Memoirs of the Lewis Family, 1850-1930.* Oxford: Leeborough Press, 1933, privately printed.

Longfellow, Henry Wadsworth. *Saga of King Olaf.*

MacDonald, George. *Phantastes.* 1858; reprint. Grand Rapids, Mich.: William B. Eerdman's Publishing Co., 1895.

Milton, John. *Paradise Lost,* 1667.

Moynihan, Martin. *The Latin Letters of C. S. Lewis.* Wheaton, Ill.: Crossway Books, 1987.

Nesbit, E. *The Amulet.* 1906.

O'Connor, Frank, ed. *Book of Ireland.* William Collins Co., 1959.

Potter, Beatrix. *Squirrel Nutkin.* 1903.

Sayer, George. *Jack.* Wheaton, Ill.: Crossway Books, 1988.

Schofield, Stephen, ed. *In Search of C. S. Lewis.* Bridge Publishing, Inc., 1983.

Swift, Jonathan. *Gulliver's Travels.* 1726; reprint. New American Library of Literature, 1960.

Thomas, Roger. *Journey Through Wales.* Gallery Books.

Twain, Mark. *A Connecticut Yankee in King Arthur's Court.* 1889

Van Dyke, Henry. *The Blue Flower.* New York: Charles Scribners Sons, 1902.

Wagner, Richard. *Siegfried and the Twilight of the Gods.* Translated by Margaret Armour. New York: Doubleday, Page & Co., 1911.

Walsh, Chad. *Apostle to the Sceptics.* New York: Macmillan, 1949.

PHOTOS AND ILLUSTRATIONS

PHOTOS COURTESY OF THE MARION E. WADE COLLECTION:

C. S. Lewis at desk, pg. ix, C. S. Lewis, pg 21, family group, pg. 22, baby C. S. Lewis, pg. 23, family in the garden, pg. 24, Jacks with cousin and mother, pg. 25, family at the beach, pg. 27, Jack and Warren with bicycles, pg. 29, Florence Hamilton Lewis, pg. 33, Florence Hamilton Lewis, pg. 34, family group on doorstep, pg. 35, family group on vacation, pg. 36, Albert Lewis, pg. 43, Warren, father and Jack, pg. 45, Albert Lewis, pg. 47, Jack, Warren, Albert, and neighbor, pg. 73, C. S. Lewis and father, pg. 95, W. T. Kirkpatrick and wife, pg. 101, Jack and Paddy, pg. 103, C. S. Lewis and Warren, pg. 107, C. S. Lewis, David, and Doug Gresham, pg. 125 and C. S. Lewis, pg. 133.

PHOTO COURTESY OF PUBLIC RECORD OFFICE OF NORTHERN IRELAND:

C. S. Lewis, pg. 19, pg. 69.

PHOTOS COURTESY OF EDWARD A. CORDING:

The River Wye, pg. 39, Ruldlau Castle, pg. 39, Brecon Beacons, pg. 40, Capel Curig, pg. 40, Teifi River, pg. 46, and Magdalen College, pg. 107.

PHOTOS COURTESY OF RUTH CORDING:

Bodleian Tower, pg. 45, Radcliffe Camera, pg. 97, and Blackwell's Books, pg. 102.

PHOTOS COURTESY OF ROBERT CORDING:

Irish tea, pg. vii, Little Lea, pg. xiii, Bible, pg. xv, Little Lea, pg. 21, the Promenade, pg. 27, gramophone and shovel, pg. 28, shovel, pgs. 30, 31, knitting, pg. 32, gloves, pg. 33, St. Mark's Rectory, pg. 35, St. Marks Church, pg. 37, bread, pg. 38, rectory sign, pg. 41, shaving brush, pg. 42, glasses and books, pg. 43, Bowler hat and book, pg. 47, Belmont Avenue, pg. 48, Belfast skyline, pg. 49, Castlerock, pg. 51, farmhouse, pg. 51, sea shells, pg. 52, post office, pg. 52, shoreline, pg. 53, shoreline, pg. 54, Salmon cottage, pg. 55, Ballintoy Harbour, pg. 60, Castlerock dunes, pg. 62, Larne Harbour, pg. 64, downtown Ballycastle, pg. 65, flowers, pg. 66, Little Lea, pg. 67, staircase, pg. 69, Belfast, pg. 72, harbor view, pg. 73, books, pg. 79, window, pg. 91, Campbell College, pg. 96, High Street, pg. 98, Magdalen Tower, pg. 100, Magdalen College, pg. 103, Kilns, pg. 104, trees, pg. 105, Deer Park gate, pg. 106, punts, pg. 108, Centenary statue, pg. 111, Lewis books, pg. 111, Six Bells Pub, pg. 122, Kilns doorway, pg. 125, The Kilns, pg. 126, 127, Parish Church, pg. 129, Lewis grave, pg. 129, and Kiln Lane, pg. 130.

Ruth Cording photo, pg. 141, courtesy, Tony Francis Photography.

ILLUSTRATIONS:

Gulliver's Travels, C. Morten adapted, pg. 79, Sir Nigel, adapted, pg. 80, Knight, RPC adapted, pg. 81, Gulliver's Travels, C. Morten adapted, pg. 82, Connecticut Yankee, Henry Pitz, adapted, pg. 83, Horse and Knight, RPC adapted, pg. 85, Balder, RPC adapted, pg. 87, and Water Babies, adapted, pg. 89.

RUTH JAMES CORDING

is a freelance writer living in Wheaton, Illinois. She is a member of The National League of American Pen Women, Chicago Branch.

Her beloved husband, Edward A. Cording, of sixty-two years, was executive director of the Conservatory of Music of Wheaton College for many years; professor emeritus, he died August 12, 1997.

A graduate of Wheaton College, Ruth Cording has served as college archivist, special instructor in children's literature, and for many years assisted in the establishing of the C. S. Lewis Collection at Wheaton College, now known as the Wade Center, featuring the works of seven British authors. It has become the most comprehensive C. S. Lewis collection in the world, with some twelve hundred of his letters and all of his books.

The Ruth James Cording Welsh Language and Literature Collection was opened March 1993, in the Special Collections of the Buswell Library, Wheaton College.

She received the Distinguished Service to Alma Mater Award from Wheaton College in October 1996.

Ruth Cording is the mother of three adult children: Dr. Edward J. Cording, consultant and professor of civil engineering at the University of Illinois, Urbana; Robert P. Cording, artist and film producer in California; and Dr. Margaret Cording Petty, professor of music with Greater Europe Mission, Lamorlaye, France.

Ruth's paternal grandparents came from Wales more than a century ago. Maternal grandparents were of English and Irish descent.

Books authored by Ruth Cording

The Joy of Remembering Special Friends
(Anderson, Ind.: Warner Press)

The Joy of Remembering Our Guests
(Anderson, Ind.: Warner Press)

The Joy of Remembering Our Children
(Anderson, Ind.: Warner Press)

Romance, Roses, and Responsibility
(Wheaton, Ill.: Wheaton College
Women's Club)

The Turquoise Bracelet
(Chicago, Ill.: Moody Press)

Glenn and Bill at Prospect Point
(Chicago, Ill.: Moody Press)

Feature Articles by Ruth Cording

The Links of the Inklings (Riverside,
Calif.: Mythopoeic Society)

A History of The Wade Center
(Wheaton College, Wade Center)

Billy Graham, Chosen of God
(Wheaton Alumni magazine)

God Gets the Royalties: Ken Taylor
(Wheaton Alumni magazine)

A Cameo of Adeline Eliza Collins,
Wheaton's First Alumna
(Wheaton Alumni magazine)

143

ROBERT CORDING

The photography (as indicated), illustrations, and design concept of *C. S. Lewis, A Celebration of His Early Life* is by Robert Cording, a freelance artist and film producer.

In 1984, he was instrumental in purchasing The Kilns, the home of C. S. Lewis, and establishing a partnership to secure it for research and historical purposes.